COMPUTER NETWORKS

BASICS OF NETWORKING

PROF. RAHENAAZ PATHAN

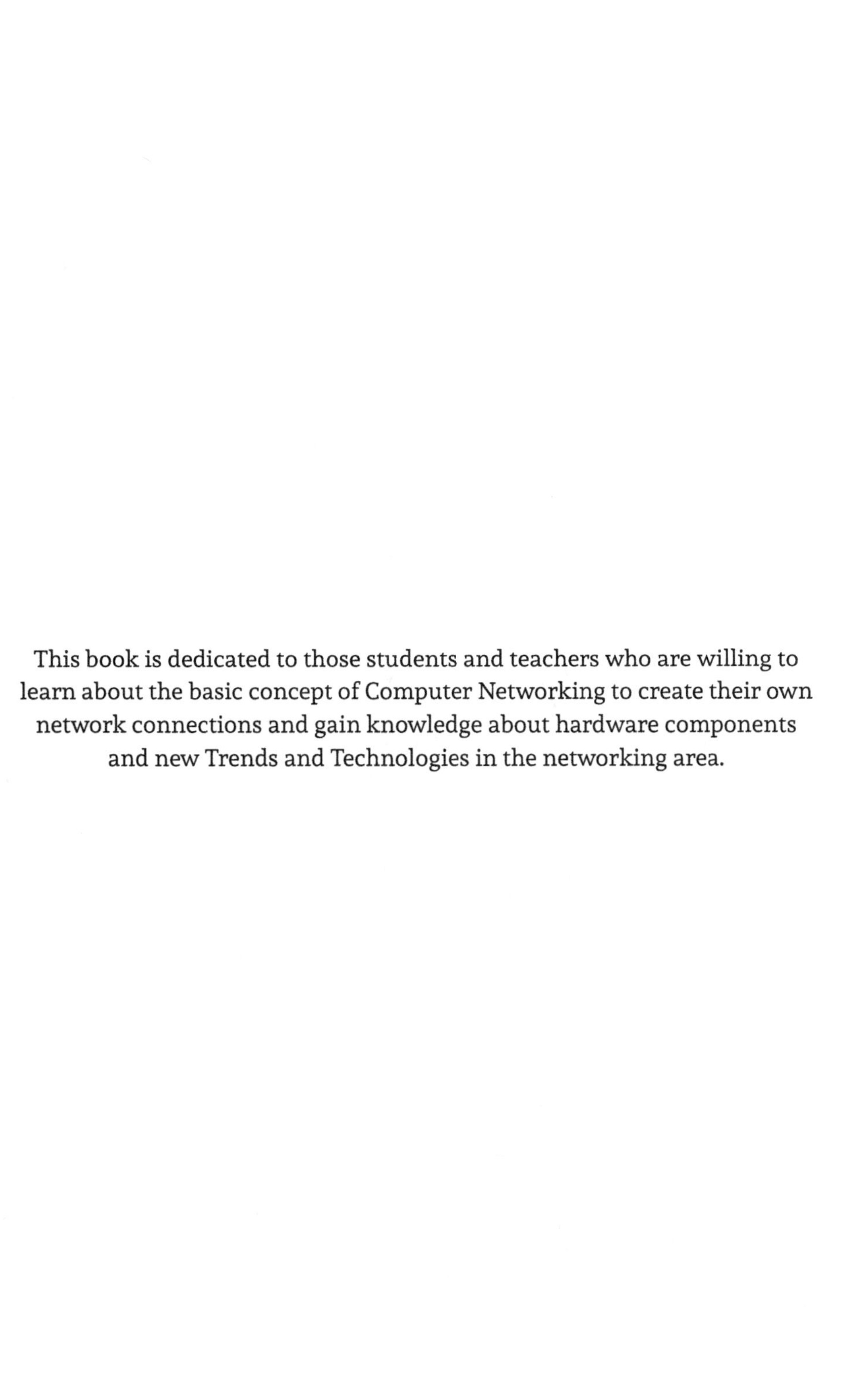

This book is dedicated to those students and teachers who are willing to learn about the basic concept of Computer Networking to create their own network connections and gain knowledge about hardware components and new Trends and Technologies in the networking area.

Contents

Foreword

If you want to learn any trend and technologies and you are willing to create any hardware and software application you need to clear your basic concepts of that particular domain. The Computer network is useful to create connection between many devices and connected applications. You can gain the concepts with different networking strategy with different concepts.

This book fully embraces the potential of the Computer Networks to empower its users. It's a friendly and approachable text intended to help you level up not just your knowledge of basic Networking, but also reach your confidence as a developer for new trends in general. So dive in and get ready to learn - and welcome to the Networking community.

- Prof. Rahenaaz Pathan

Preface

This book is for computer scientists,computer engineers and others who wants to learn about basic concepts of Networking area.

Our aim is to explain the enduring concepts underlying all computer system, and to show you the concrete ways that these ideas affect the correctness, performance, and utility of your application programs.This book is written from a devloper's , Networking concepts and knowledge perspective.

If you study and learn the concepts in this book, you will be on your way to becoming the rare "power developer" who knows how things work and how to fix them. Our aim is to present the fundamental concepts in ways that you will find useful right away. You will also be prepared to studying such topics as networking models , protocols and its connection based topologies.

Acknowledgements

I would like to express my greatest appreciation to the all individuals who have helped and supported me throughout writing this book. I am thankful to my family members and my colleagues during this book writing for initial advice, and encouragement, which led to the final completion of the book.

I special acknowledgment goes to my motivators Mrs. Hetal Bhaidasna who helped me in completing the book by exchanging interesting ideas and sharing their experience. Also i like to thanks to Parul University from where i got the uncountable and a lot of knowledge.

I would like to thank my special one who always motivated me to do my best in my career also Thank you for always believing in me.

I wish to thank my parents as well for their undivided support and interest who inspired me and encouraged me to go my own way, without whom I would be unable to complete this book.

In the end, I want to thank my friends who displayed appreciation for my work and motivated me to continue my work.

- Prof. Rahenaaz Pathan

Prologue

In this book the basic details of Computer Networks is given and it is starting from the basic computer networking and about networking advantages and Disadvantages as well as about architecture and protocols of networking.

Before learning the concepts of networking you aware about some basic Hardware and protocols as well as about some networking connection and security.

It has different versions can exist side by side. It is also Type safe and provides rich libraries of many built in functions.

Using Computer networks you can create new trending smart systems with security.

I

Basics of Computer Networks

What is a Computer Network and write characteristics of it?

- A computer network is a system in which multiple computers are connected to each other to share information and resources.
- The Physical connection between networked computing devices is established using either cable media or wireless media.
- The best-known computer network is the Internet.

A list Of Computer network characteristics is given below.

- Communication speed
- File sharing
- Back up and Rollback is easy
- Software and Hardware sharing
- Security
- Scalability
- Reliability

Computer Network

- Communication speed: The network provides us to communicate over the network in a fast and efficient manner. For example, we can do video conferencing, email messaging, etc. over the internet. Therefore, the computer network is a great way to share our knowledge and ideas.
- File sharing: File sharing is one of the major advantage of the computer network. Computer network provides us to share the files with each other.
- Back up and Roll back is easy : Since the files are stored in the main server which is centrally located. Therefore, it is easy to take the back up from the main server.
- Software and Hardware sharing : We can install the applications on the main server, therefore, the user can access the applications centrally. So, we do not need to install the software on every machine. Similarly, hardware can also be shared.
- Security: Network allows the security by ensuring that the user has the right to access certain files and applications.
- Scalability: Scalability means that we can add new components to the network. The network must be scalable so that we can extend the network by adding new devices. But, it decreases the speed of the connection, and data of the transmission speed also decreases, this increases the chances of an error occurring. This problem can be overcome by using routing or switching devices.

- Reliability: A computer network can use an alternative source for data communication in case of any hardware failure.

Write advantages and disadvantages of Computer Network:

Advantages:

- File sharing: The major advantage of a computer network is that is allows file sharing and remote file access. A person sitting at one workstation connected to a network can easily see files present on another workstation, provided he is authorized to do so. Resource sharing
- All computers in the network can share resources such as printers, fax machines, modems, and scanners.
- Better connectivity and communications: It allows users to connect and communicate with each other easily. Various communication applications including e-mail and groupware are used. Through e-mail, members of a network can send messages and ensure the safe delivery of data to other members, even in their absence.
- Internet access: Computer networks provide internet service over the entire network. Every single computer attached to the network can experience high-speed internet. Entertainment: Many games and other means of entertainment are easily available on the internet. Furthermore, Local Area Networks (LANs) offer and facilitates other ways of enjoyment, such as many players are connected through LAN and play a particular game with each other from a remote location.
- Inexpensive system: Shared resources mean a reduction in hardware costs. Shared files mean a reduction in memory requirement, which indirectly means a reduction in file storage expenses. A particular software can be installed only once on the server and made available across all connected computers at once. This saves the expense of buying and installing the same software as many times for as many users.
- Flexible access: A user can log on to a computer anywhere on the network and access his files. This offers flexibility to the user as to where he should be during the course of his routine.
- Instant and multiple access: Computer networks are multiply processed many of users can access the same information at the same time.

Immediate commands such as printing commands can be made with the help of computer networks.

Disadvantages :

- Lack of data security and privacy: Because there would be a huge number of people who would be using a computer network to get and share some of their files and resources, a certain user's security would be always at risk. There might even be illegal activities that would occur, which you need to be careful about and aware of.
- Presence of computer viruses and malware: If even one computer on a network gets affected by a virus, there is a possible threat for the other systems getting affected too. Viruses can spread on a network easily, because of the inter-connectivity of workstations. Moreover, multiple systems with common resources are the perfect breeding ground for viruses that multiply.
- Lack of Independence: Since most networks have a centralized server and dependent clients, the client users lack any freedom whatsoever. Centralized decision-making can sometimes hinder how a client user wants to use his own computer.
- Lack of Robustness: As previously stated, if a computer network's main server breaks down, the entire system would become useless. Also, if it has a bridging device or a central linking server that fails, the entire network would also come to a standstill.
- Need an efficient handler: For a computer network to work efficiently and optimally, it requires high technical skills and know-how of its operations and administration. A person just having basic skills cannot do this job. Take note that the responsibility to handle such a system is high, as allotting permissions and passwords can be daunting. Similarly, network configuration and connection is very tedious and cannot be done by an average technician who does not have advanced knowledge.

Write applications OR uses of Computer networks?

- Financial services: Nowadays, almost all financial services depend on the computer network. You can access financial services across the world.

For example, a user can transfer money from one place to another by using the electronic fund transfer feature.

- Business: Nowadays, most of the work of businesses is done over computers. To exchange data and ideas, you need effective data and resources sharing features. To do this, you need to connect the computer with each other through a network.
- Email services: A computer network provides you the facility to send or receive mails across the globe in few seconds.
- Mobile applications: By using the mobile applications, such as cellular or wireless phones, you can communicate (exchange your views and ideas) with one other.
- Directory services: It provides you the facility to store files on a centralized location to increase the speed of search operations worldwide.
- Teleconferencing: It contains voice conferencing and video conferencing which are based in networking. In teleconferencing, the participants need not to be presented at the same location.

Difference between LAN, MAN, and WAN:

Parameter	LAN	MAN	WAN
Area covered	Covers small area. i.e.within building	Covers larger than LAN & smaller than WAN	Covers large area
Error rates	Lowest	Moderate	Highest
Transmission speed	High speed	Moderate speed	Low speed
Equipment cost	Inexpensive	Moderate expensive	Most expensive
Design & maintenance	Easy	Moderate	Difficult

Define protocol and explain important elements of it?

- A protocol is a set of rules that governs (manages) data communications.
- Protocols defines methods of communication, how to communicate, when to communicate etc.
- A protocol is an agreement between the communicating parties on how communication is to proceed.
- Important elements of protocols are:

  1.Syntax
  2.Semantics
  3.Timing

- Syntax:- Syntax means format of data or the structure how it is presented e.g. first eight bits arefor sender address, next eight bits are for receiver address and rest of the bits for message data.
- Semantics:- Semantics is the meaning of each section of bits e.g. the address bit means theroute of transmission or final destination of message.
- Timing:- Timing means, at what time data can be sent and how fast data can be sent.
- Some protocols also support message acknowledgement and data compression designed for reliable and/or high-performance network communication.
- Example: HTTP, IP, FTP etc...

Define OSI model and explain function of each layer?

- OSI model is based on a proposal developed by the International Standards Organization (ISO) as a first step toward international standardization of the protocols used in the various layers.
- It was revised in 1995.
- The model is called the OSI (Open Systems Interconnection) Reference Model because it deals with connecting open systems—that is, systems

that are open for communication with other systems.
- The OSI model has seven layers:

  - Physical Layer
  - Data Link Layer
  - Network Layer
  - Transport Layer
  - Session Layer
  - Presentation Layer
  - Application Layer

Physical layer (layer 1): OSI Model, Layer 1 conveys the bit stream - electrical impulse, light or radio signal through the network at the electrical and mechanical level. It provides the hardware means of sending and receiving data on a carrier, including defining cables, cards and physical aspects. RS232, and ATM are protocols with physical layer components.

Layer 1 Physical examples include Ethernet, FDDI, B8ZS, V.35, V.24, RJ45.

Data Link (Layer 2): At OSI Model, Layer 2, data packets are encoded and decoded into bits. It furnishes protocol knowledge and management and handles errors in the physical layer, flow control and frame synchronization. The data link layer is divided into two sub layers: The Media Access Control layer and the logical link control layer. The MAC sub layer controls how a computer on the network gains access to the data and permission to transmit it. The LLC layer controls frame syncronization, flow control and error checking. Layer 2 Data Link examples include PPP, FDDI, ATM, IEEE 802.5/ 802.2, IEEE 802.3/802.2, HDLC, Frame Relay.

Network (Layer 3): Layer 3 provides switiching and routingtechnologies, creating logical paths, known as vitual circuits , for transmitting data from node to node. Routing and forwarding are functions of this layer, as well as addressing, error handling, and packet sequencing. Layer 3 Network examples include AppleTalk DDP, IP, IPX.

Transport (Layer 4): OSI Model, Layer 4, provides transparent transfer of data between end systems, or hosts, and is responsible for end-to-end error recovery and flow control. It ensures complete data transfer.

Layer 4 Transport examples include SPX, TCP, UDP.

Session (Layer 5): This layer establishes, manages and terminates connections between applications The session layer sets up, coordinates, and terminates conversations, exchanges, and dialogues between the applications at each end. It deals with session and connection coordination.

Presentation (Layer 6): This layer provides independence from differences in data representation (e.g., encryption) by translating from application to network format, and vice versa. The presentation layer works to transform data into the form that the

application layer can accept. This layer formats and encrypts data to be sent across a network, providing freedom from compatibility problems. It is sometimes called the syntax layer.

Layer 6 Presentation examples include encryption, ASCII, EBCDIC, TIFF, GIF, PICT, JPEG, MPEG, and MIDI.

Application (Layer 7): OSI Model, Layer 7, supports Application and end-user processes. Communication partners are identified, quality of service is identified, user authentication and privacy are considered, and any constraints on data Syntax are identified. Everything at this layer is application-specific. This layer provides application services for file transfers, e-MAIL, and other network softwareservices. Telnet and FTP are applications that exist entirely at the application level. Tiered application architectures are part of this layer.

Layer 7 Application examples include WWW browsers, NFS, SNMP, Telnet, HTTP, FTP

TCP/IP (Internet Protocol Stack layers) Reference Model and explain function of each layer?

- Transmission Control Protocol/Internet Protocol (TCP/IP) protocol suite is the engine for the Internet and networks worldwide.
- TCP/IP either combines several OSI layers into a single layer, or does not use certain layers at all
- TCP/IP is a set of protocols developed to allow cooperating computers to share resources across the network.
- The TCP/IP model has five layers.

  - Application Layer
  - Transport Layer
  - Internet Layer
  - Data Link Layer
  - Physical Layer

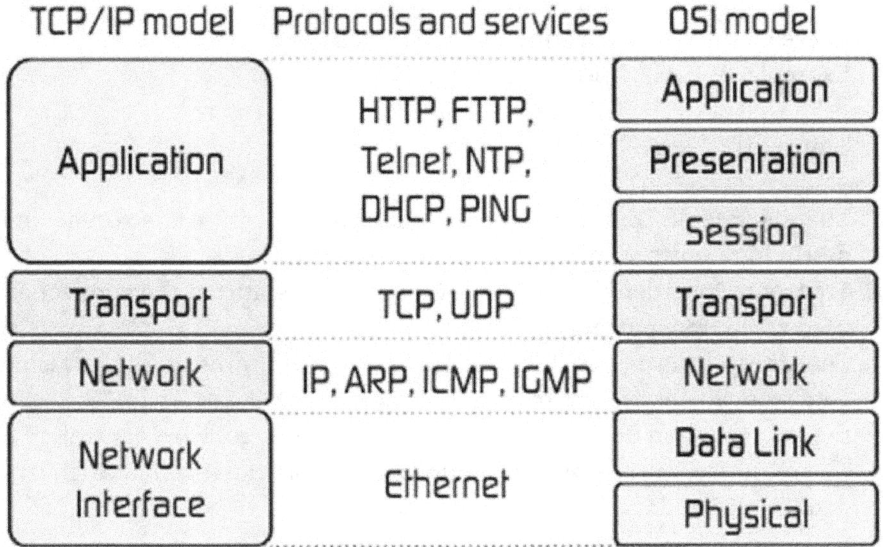

TCP/IP Reference Model

Physical and Data link layer:

- The function of the Physical and Data link layer is the same as the OSI model.

Network Layer (Internet Layer):

- The internet layer is also called the network layer.
- Internet layer pack data into data packets known as IP datagrams, which contain source and destination address (logical address or IP address) information that is used to forward the datagrams between hosts and across networks.
- The Internet layer is also responsible for the routing of IP datagrams.
- Internet Protocol (IP) is the most important protocol in this layer.
- It is a connectionless protocol that does not assume reliability from lower layers. IP does not provide reliability, flow control or error recovery.

- IP provides a routing function that attempts to deliver transmitted messages to their destination.
- These message units in an IP network are called an IP datagram.
- Example: IP, ICMP, IGMP, ARP, and RARP

Transport Layer:

- The purpose of Transport layer is to permit devices on the source and destination hosts to carry on a conversation.
- Transport layer defines the level of service and status of the connection used when transporting data.
- The transport layer provides the end-to-end data transfer by delivering data from an application to its remote peer.
- the Transmission Control protocol Congestion control Flow control
- The most-used transport layer Protocol (TCP), provides: Reliable delivery data Duplicate data suppression

Application layer :

- As we can see from the above figure, presentation and session layers are not there in TCP/IP model. Also, note that the Network Access Layer in TCP/IP model combines the functions of Data link Layer and Physical Layer.
- Application layer is the top most layer of four-layer TCP/IP model.
- Application layer is present on the top of the Transport layer.
- Application layer defines TCP/IP application protocols and how host programs interface with Transport layer services to use the network.
- Application layer includes all the higher-level protocols like DNS (Domain Naming System), HTTP (Hypertext Transfer Protocol), Telnet, SSH, FTP (File Transfer Protocol), TFTP (Trivial File Transfer Protocol), SNMP (Simple Network Management Protocol), SMTP (Simple Mail Transfer Protocol), DHCP (Dynamic Host Configuration Protocol), X Windows, RDP (Remote Desktop Protocol) etc.

Network Interface Layer (Network Access Layer):

- Network Access Layer defines details of how data is physically sent through the network, including how bits are electrically or optically

signaled by hardware devices that interface directly with a network medium, such as coaxial cable, optical fiber, or twisted pair copper wire.
* The protocols included in Network Access Layer are Ethernet, Token Ring, FDDI, X.25, Frame Relay, etc.

Difference between OSI and TCP/IP model?

TCP/IP	OSI Model
The full form of TCP/IP is Transmission Control Protocol/ Internet Protocol	The full form of OSI is Open Systems Interconnection
It is a communication protocol that is based on standard protocols and allows the connection of hosts over a network	It is a structured model which deals which the functioning of a network
In 1982, the TCP/IP model became the standard language of ARPANET	In 1984, the OSI model was introduced by the International Organisation of Standardization (ISO)
It comprises of four layers: • Network Interface • Internet • Transport • Application	It comprises seven layers: • Physical • Data Link • Network • Transport • Session • Presentation • Application
It follows a horizontal approach	It follows a vertical approach
The TCP/IP is the implementation of the OSI Model	An OSI Model is a reference model, based on which a network is created
It is protocol dependent	It is protocol independent

Difference between Connection-Oriented and Connectionless services?

BASIS OF COMPARISON	CONNECTION-ORIENTED SERVICE	CONNECTION-LESS SERVICE
Prior Connection Requirement	Necessary	Not required
Reliability	Ensures reliable transfer of data.	Not guaranteed.
Congestion	Unlikely	Occur likely.
Transferring mode	It can be implemented using circuit switching and virtual circuit.	It is implemented using packet switching.
Lost data retransmission	Feasible	Practically, not possible.
Suitability	Suitable for long and steady communication.	Suitable for bursty Transmission.
Signaling	Used for connection establishment.	There is no concept of signaling.
Packet forwarding	Packets sequentially travel to their destination node and follows the same route	Packets reach the destination randomly without following the same route.

II

Transmission Media

List out types of guided media.

- Twisted Pair Cable.
- Co-axial Cable.
- Power Lines.
- Fibre Optic Cable.

Draw a Transmission media chart.

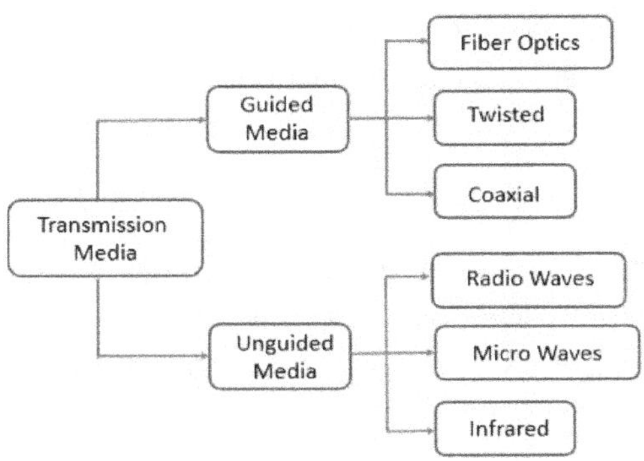

Transmission Media chart

Explain co-axial cable in detail.

A Coaxial cable is a cable used in the transmission of video, communications, and audio. This cable has high bandwidths and greater transmission capacity. Most users relate to a coaxial or coax cable as a cable used to connect their TVs to a cable TV service. However, these cables are also used in networks and what allows a broadband cable Internet connection using a cable modem.

There are two types of coaxial cable:

- Thinnet cable (10Base2)
- Thicknet cable (10Base5)
- Thinnet cable (10Base2)

Thinnet coaxial cable is connected using special connectors and requires to be terminated at each end using a 50ohm resistor.

10Base2 stands for:

- Data Transmission Rate of 10Mbps, i.e. 10
- Uses baseband transmission, i.e. Base
- Used in Ethernet networks it has a maximum cable length of 185 meters, i.e. the 2 for approximately 200 meters
- Thicknet cable (10Base5):

The thicker the copper core, the further the cable can carry signals. Thicknet is sometimes used as a backbone to connect several smaller thinnet-based networks.

10base5 stands for:

- Data Transmission Rate of 10Mbps, i.e. 10
- Uses baseband transmission, i.e. Base
- Used in Ethernet networks it has a maximum cable length of 500 metres, i.e. the 5 is for 500 metres.

Benefits or advantages of Coaxial Cable
Following are the benefits or advantages of Coaxial Cable:

- Due to the skin effect, coaxial cable is used in high-frequency applications (> 50 MHz) using copper-clad materials for the center conductor. The skin effect is result of high-frequency signals propagating along the outer surface of the conductor. It increases tensile strength of the cable and reduces weight.
- The cost of a coaxial cable is less.
- The outer conductor in coaxial cable is used to improve attenuation and shield effectiveness. This can be further enhanced with the use of a second foil or braid known as a jacket (C2 as designated in the figure-1). The jacket is used as a protective cover from the environment and makes the overall coaxial cable as a flame retardant.
- It is less susceptible to noise or interference (EMI or RFI) compare to twisted pair cable. It supports high bandwidth signal transmission compare to twisted pair.
- It is easy to wire and easy to expand due to flexibility. It allows high transfer rates with coaxial cable having better shielding materials.

Drawbacks or disadvantages of Coaxial Cable, Following are the disadvantages of Coaxial Cable:

- It is bulky.
- It is expensive to install for longer distances due to its thickness and stiffness. As a single cable is used for signal transmission across the entire network, in case of failure in one cable the entire network will be down.
- Security is a great concern as it is easy to tap the coaxial cable by breaking it and inserting a T-joint (of BNC type) in between.
- It must be grounded to prevent interference.

Uses/application:

- Coaxial cable is used in cable TV connections.
- Also used by telephone companies to connect central offices to telephone poles near customer sites.
- Coaxial cables are used to connect Radio transmitters and receivers to their antennas.
- Coaxial cables are used in digital audio (S/P DIF)

Explain fiber optic cable in detail.

Fiber optic cable is a high-speed data transmission medium. It contains tiny glass or plastic filaments that carry light beams. Digital data is transmitted through the cable via rapid pulses of light.

Because fiber optic cables transmit data via light waves, they can transfer information at the speed of light. Not surprisingly, fiber optic cables provide the fastest data transfer rate of any data transmission medium.

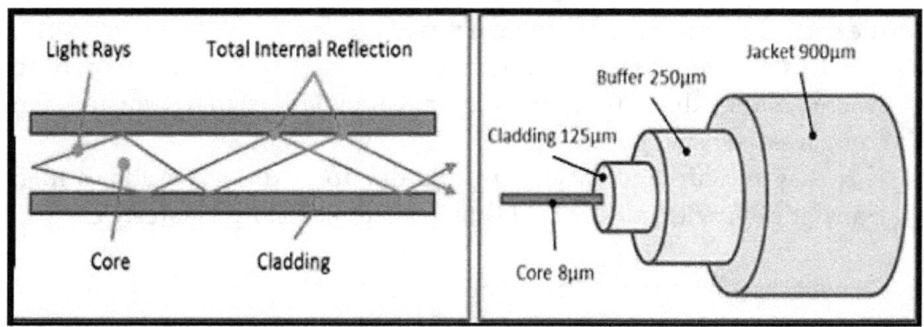

Fiber optic cable

Since fiber optic cables provide fast transfer speeds and large bandwidth, they are used for a large part of the Internet backbone.

Advantages:

Extremely High Bandwidth: No other cable-based data transmission medium offers the bandwidth that fiber does. The volume of data that fiber optic cables transmit per unit of time is far great than copper cables

Longer Distance: in fiber optic transmission, optical cables are capable of providing low power loss, which enables signals can be transmitted to a longer distance than copper cables.

Resistance to Electromagnetic Interference: in practical cable deployment, it's inevitable to meet environments like power substations, heating, ventilating, and other industrial sources of interference. However, fiber has a very low rate of bit error (10 EXP-13), as a result of fiber being so resistant to electromagnetic interference. Fiber optic transmission is virtually noise-free

Low-Security Risk: the growth of the fiber optic communication market is mainly driven by increasing awareness about data security concerns and use of the alternative raw material. Data or signals are transmitted via light in fiber optic transmission. Therefore there is no way to detect the data being transmitted by "listening in" to the electromagnetic energy "leaking" through the cable, which ensures the absolute security of information

Small Size: fiber optic cable has a very small diameter. For instance, the cable diameter of a single OM3 multimode fiber is about 2mm, which is smaller than that of a coaxial copper cable. Small size saves more space in fiber optic transmission.

Disadvantages :

Fragility: usually optical fiber cables are made of glass, which lends to they are more fragile than electrical wires. In addition, glass can be affected by various chemicals including hydrogen gas (a problem in underwater cables), making them need more care when deployed underground.

Difficult to Install: it's not easy to splice fiber optic cable. And if you bend them too much, they will break. And fiber cable is highly susceptible to becoming cut or damaged during installation or construction activities. All these make it difficult to install.

Attenuation & Dispersion: as transmission distance gets longer, the light will be attenuated and dispersed, which requires extra optical components like EDFA to be added.

Explain error control and flow control in brief:

- Flow Control mainly coordinates with the amount of data that can be sent before receiving an acknowledgment from the receiver and it is one of the major duties of the data link layer.
- For most protocols, flow control is a set of procedures that mainly tells the sender how much data the sender can send before it must wait for an acknowledgment from the receiver.
- Error Control contains both error detection and error correction. It mainly allows the receiver to inform the sender about any damaged or lost frames during the transmission and then it coordinates with the retransmission of those frames by the sender.
- The term Error control in the data link layer mainly refers to the methods of error detection and retransmission. Error control is mainly

implemented in a simple way and that is whenever there is an error detected during the exchange, then specified frames are retransmitted this process is also referred to as Automatic Repeat request(ARQ).

- The implementation of protocols is mainly implemented in the software by using one of the common programming languages. The classification of the protocols can be mainly done on the basis of where they are being used.
- Protocols can be used for noiseless channels(that is error-free) and also used for noisy channels(that is error-creating). The protocols used for noiseless channels mainly cannot be used in real-life and are mainly used to serve as the basis for the protocols used for noisy channels.
- All the above-given protocols are unidirectional in the sense that the data frames travel from one node i.e Sender to the other node i.e receiver.
- The special frames called acknowledgment (ACK) and negative acknowledgment (NAK) both can flow in opposite directions for flow and error control purposes and the data can flow in only one direction.
- But in the real-life network, the protocols of the data link layer are implemented as bidirectional which means the flow of the data is in both directions. And in these protocols, the flow control and error control information such as ACKs and NAKs are included in the data frames in a technique that is commonly known as piggybacking.
- Also, bidirectional protocols are more complex than unidirectional protocols.
- The data flow must not be allowed to overwhelm the receiver; because any receiving device has a very limited speed at which the device can process the incoming data and a limited amount of memory to store the incoming data.
- The processing rate is slower than the transmission rate; due for this reason each receiving device has a block of memory that is commonly known as a buffer, which is used to store the incoming data until this data will be processed. In case the buffer begins to fill up then the receiver must be able to tell the sender to halt the transmission until once again the receiver become able to receive.

Define Topology. Explain different types of topology.

- Network Topology is the schematic description of a network arrangement, connecting various nodes (sender and receiver) through lines of connection.
- A Network Topology is the arrangement with which computer systems or network devices are connected to each other.
- Types of network topologies :

  - Bus topology
  - Star topology
  - Mesh topology
  - Ring topology
  - Mesh topology
  - Hybrid topology
  - Star topology

Bus Topology

Bus topology is a network type in which every computer and network device is connected to a single cable.

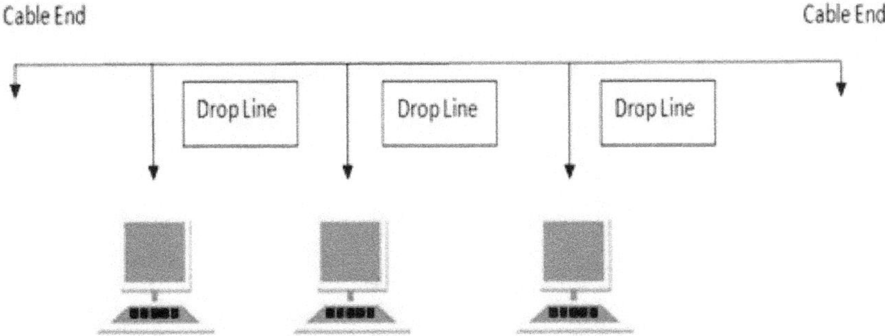

Bus Topology

Features:

- It transmits data only in one direction.
- Every device is connected to a single cable.

Advantages :

- It is cost-effective (cheaper).
- The cable required is the least compared to other network topologies.
- Used in small networks.
- It is easy to understand.
- Easy to expand joining two cables together.

Disadvantages :

- Cables fail then the whole network fails.
- If network traffic is heavy or nodes are more the performance of the network decreases.
- Cable has a limited length.

Ring Topology

- It is called ring topology because it forms a ring as each computer is connected to another computer, with the last one connected to the first. Exactly two neighbors for each device.

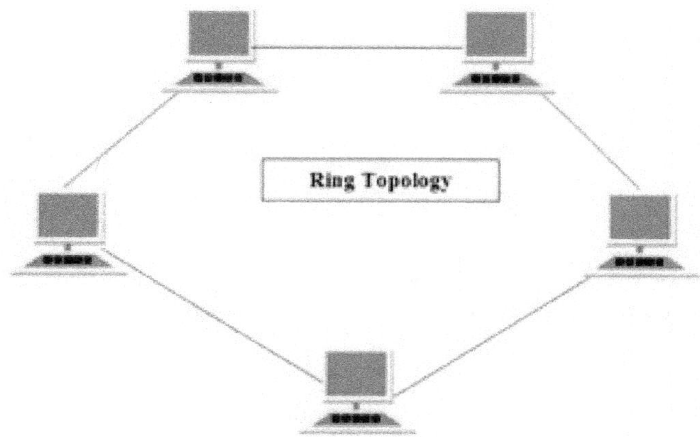

Ring Topology

Features:

- A number of repeaters are used and the transmission is unidirectional.

- Data is transferred in a sequential manner that is bit by bit.

Advantages:

- The transmitting network is not affected by high traffic or by adding more nodes, as only the nodes having tokens can transmit data.
- Cheap to install and expand.
- Troubleshooting is difficult in a ring topology.

Disadvantages:

- Adding or deleting the computers disturbs the network activity.
- Failure of one computer disturbs the whole network.

Star Topology

In this type of topology, all the computers are connected to a single hub through a cable. This hub is the central node and all others nodes are connected to the central node.

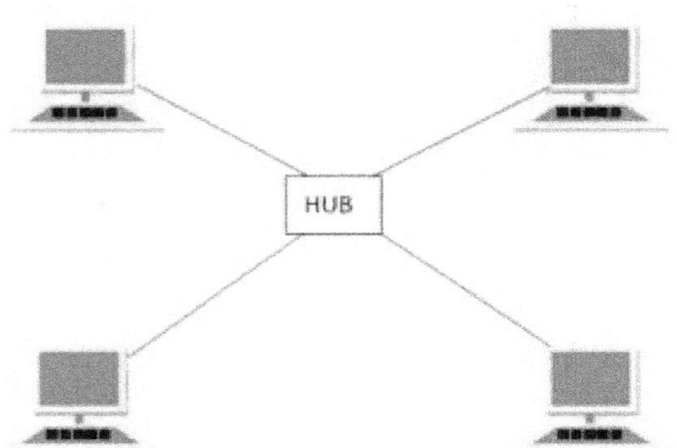

Star Topology

Features:

- Every node has its own dedicated connection to the hub.
- Acts as a repeater for data flow.

- Can be used with a twisted pair, Optical Fibre, or coaxial cable.

Advantages:

- Fast performance with few nodes and low network traffic.
- Hub can be upgraded easily.
- Easy to troubleshoot.
- Easy to set up and modify.
- Only that node is affected which has failed rest of the nodes can work smoothly.

Disadvantages:

- The cost of installation is high.
- Expensive to use.
- If the hub is affected then the whole network is stopped because all the nodes depend on the hub.

Mesh Topology

It is a point-to-point connection to other nodes or devices.

Traffic is carried only between two devices or nodes to which it is connected.

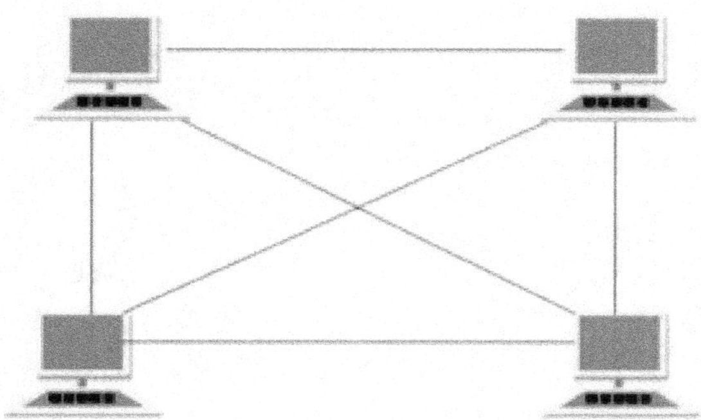

Mesh Topology

Features:

- Fully connected.
- Robust.
- Not flexible.

Advantages:

- Each connection can carry its own data load.
- It is robust.

Disadvantages:

- Installation and configuration is difficult.
- Cabling cost is more.
- Bulk wiring is required.
- Fault is diagnosed easily.
- Provides security and privacy.

Tree Topology

- It has a root node and all other nodes are connected to it forming a hierarchy.
- It is also called hierarchical topology.
- It should at least have three levels to the hierarchy.

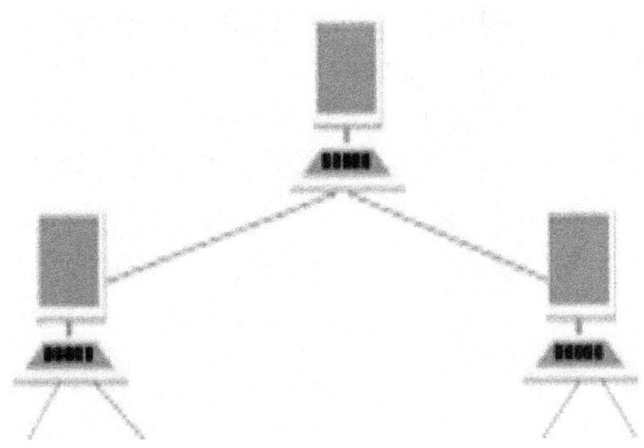

Tree Topology

Features:

- Ideal if workstations are located in groups.
- Used in Wide Area Network.
- Extension of bus and star topologies.
- Expansion of nodes is possible and easy.
- Easily managed and maintained.
- Error detection is easily done.

Advantages:

- Extension of bus and star topologies.
- Expansion of nodes is possible and easy.
- Easily managed and maintained.
- Error detection is easily done.

Disadvantages:

- Heavily cabled.
- Costly.
- If more nodes are added maintenance is difficult.
- If the central hub fails then the network fails.

Hybrid Topology

- A network structure whose design contains more than one topology is said to be hybrid topology. For example, if in an office in one department ring topology is used and in another star topology is used, connecting these topologies will result in Hybrid Topology (ring topology and star topology).

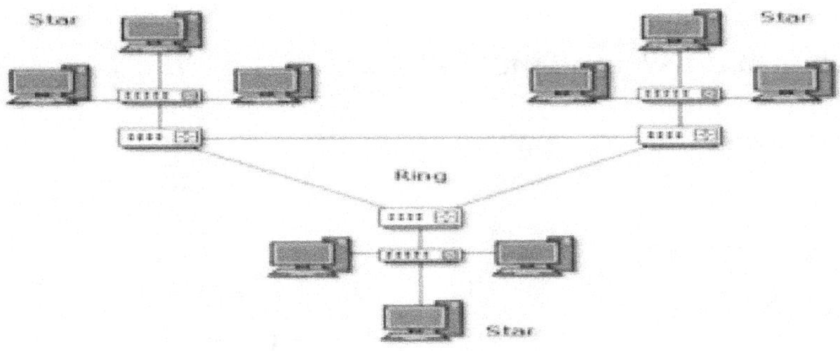

Hybrid Topology

Features:

- It is a combination of two or more topologies
- Inherits the advantages and disadvantages of the topologies included

Advantages:

- Reliable as error detecting and trouble shooting is easy.
- Scalable as size can be increased easily.
- Flexible.

Disadvantages:

- Cost Is Higher Than Copper Cable: despite the fact that fiber optic installation costs are dropping by as much as 60% a year, installing fiber optic cabling is still relatively higher than copper cables. Because copper cable installation does not need extra care like fiber cables.
- Complex in design.
- Costly.

Explain wireless transmission media with example:

Microwaves Transmission:

Microwaves are of two types:

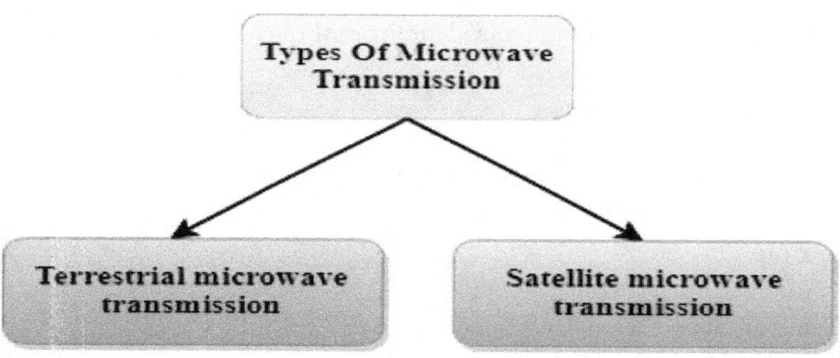

Terrestrial Microwave Transmission: A focused beam of a radio signal is sent from one ground-based microwave transmission antenna to another using terrestrial microwave transmission. Microwaves are electromagnetic waves that range in frequency from 1GHz to 1000 GHz. Microwaves are unidirectional as the sending and receiving antenna is to be aligned, i.e., the waves sent by the sending antenna are narrowly focused. In this case, antennas are mounted on the towers to send a beam to another antenna that is km away and works on line of sight transmission.

Characteristics of Microwave:

- Frequency range: The frequency range of terrestrial microwave is from 4-6 GHz to 21-23 GHz.
- Bandwidth: It supports the bandwidth from 1 to 10 Mbps.
- Short distance: It is inexpensive for short distance.
- Long distance: It is expensive as it requires a higher tower for a longer distance.
- Attenuation: Attenuation means loss of signal. It is affected by environmental conditions and antenna size.

Advantages Of Microwave:

- Microwave transmission is cheaper than using cables.
- It is free from land acquisition as it does not require any land for the installation of cables.
- Microwave transmission provides an easy communication in terrains as the installation of cable in terrain is quite a difficult task.
- Communication over oceans can be achieved by using microwave transmission.

Disadvantages of Microwave transmission:

- Eavesdropping: An eavesdropping creates insecure communication. Any malicious user can catch the signal in the air by using its own antenna.
- Out of phase signal: A signal can be moved out of phase by using microwave transmission.
- Susceptible to weather condition: A microwave transmission is susceptible to weather condition. This means that any environmental change such as rain, wind can distort the signal.
- Bandwidth limited: Allocation of bandwidth is limited in the case of microwave transmission.

Explain Radio Waves in brief:

Radio waves uses are explained in correspondence than other electromagnetic waves primarily in light of their attractive proliferation properties, coming from their enormous radio waves wavelength. Radio waves wavelength can go through the atmosphere, foliage, and most structure materials, and by diffraction can twist around blocks, and not at all like other electromagnetic waves, they will, in general, be dissipated instead of consumed by objects bigger than their frequency of radio waves.

Radio waves use are found in standard communicate radio and TV, shortwave radio, route and airport regulation, cell communication, and even remote-controlled toys.

It is a technique where data is transmitted using radio waves and therefore energy travels through the air rather than copper or glass. Conceptually, radio, TV, cellular phones etc. uses radio transmission in one form or another.

The radio waves can travel through walls and through an entire building. Depending upon the frequency, they can travel long distance or short distance. Satellite relay is the one example of long distance communication.

Therefore, each frequency range is divided into different bands, which has a specific range of frequencies in the radio frequency, (RF) spectrum. The RF is divided in different ranges starting from very low frequencies (VLF) to extremely high frequencies (EHF). Figure shows , each band with a defined upper and lower frequency "limit.

The basic features of the radio waves are that:

- they are easy to generate
- they have same velocity in vacuum
- they may traverse long distances
- they are omni-directional
- they can penetrate building easily so they find extensive use in communication both indoor and outdoor
- they are frequency dependent. At low frequency they can pass through obstacles well but the power falls off sharply With distance from the source, as power is inversely proportional to cube of the distance from the source. At HF they travel in straight lines and bounce off obstacles.

Explain Infrared in brief:

infrared technology uses diffuse light reflected at walls, furniture etc. or a directed light if a line of sight (LOS) exists between sender and receiver.

Infrared light is the part of the electromagnetic spectrum, and is an electromagnetic form of radiation. It comes from the heat and thermal radiation, and it is not visible to the naked eyes.

In infrared transmission, senders can be simple light emitting diodes (LEDs) or laser diodes. Photodiodes act as receivers.

Infrared is used in wireless technology devices or systems that convey data through infrared radiation. Infrared is electromagnetic energy at a wave length or wave lengths somewhat longer than those of red light.

Infrared wireless is used for medium and short range communications and control. Infrared technology is used in instruction detectors; robot control system, medium range line of sight laser communication, cordless microphone, headsets, modems, and other peripheral devices.

Infrared radiation is used in scientific, industrial, and medical application. Night vision devices using active near infrared illumination allow people and animals to be observed without the observer being detected.

Infrared transmission technology refers to energy in the region of the electromagnetic radiation spectrum at wavelength longer than those of visible light but shorter than those of radio waves.

Infrared technology allows computing devices to communicate via short range wireless signals. With infrared transmission, computers can transfer files and other digital data bidirectional.

Advantages of infrared : The main advantage of infrared technology is its simple and extremely cheap senders and receivers which are integrated into nearly all mobile devices available today. No licenses are required for infrared and shielding is very simple. PDAs, laptops, notebooks, mobile phones etc. have an infrared data association (IrDA) interface. Electrical devices cannot interfere with infrared transmission.

Disadvantages of Infrared: Disadvantages of infrared transmission are its low bandwidth compared to other LAN technologies. Limited transfer rates to 115 Kbit/s and we know that even 4 Mbit/s is not a particular high data rate. Their main disadvantage is that infrared is quite easily shielded. Infrared transmission cannot penetrate walls or other obstacles.

III
Network Layer

Explain Design issues in network layer.

<u>Network layer</u> is majorly focused on getting packets from the source to the destination, routing error handling and congestion control.

Before learning about design issues in the network layer, let's learn about it's various functions.

<u>Addressing</u>:

Maintains the address at the frame header of both source and destination and performs addressing to detect various devices in network.

Packeting:

This is performed by Internet Protocol. The network layer converts the packets from its upper layer.

<u>Routing</u>:

It is the most important functionality. The network layer chooses the most relevant and best path for the data transmission from source to destination.

Inter-networking:

It works to deliver a logical connection across multiple devices.

Network layer design issues:

The network layer comes with some design issues they are described as follows:

1. Store and Forward packet switching:The host sends the packet to the nearest router. This packet is stored there until it has fully arrived once the link is fully processed by verifying the checksum then it is forwarded to the next router till it reaches the destination. This mechanism is called "Store

and Forward packet switching."

2. Services provided to <u>Transport Layer</u>:Through the network/transport layer interface, the network layer transfers it's services to the transport layer. These services are described below.

But before providing these services to the transfer layer following goals must be kept in mind :- Offering services must not depend on router technology. The transport layer needs to be protected from the type, number and topology of the available router.

The network addresses for the transport layer should use uniform numbering pattern also at LAN and WAN connections.

Based on the connections there are 2 types of services provided :

Connectionless – The routing and insertion of packets into subnet is done individually. No added setup is required.

Connection-Oriented – Subnet must offer reliable service and all the packets must be transmitted over a single route.

3. Implementation of <u>Connectionless Service</u>:

Packet are termed as "datagrams" and corresponding subnet as "datagram subnets". When the message size that has to be transmitted is 4 times the size of the packet, then the network layer divides into 4 packets and transmits each packet to router via. a few protocol. Each data packet has destination address and is routed independently irrespective of the packets.

4. Implementation of Connection Oriented service:

To use a connection-oriented service, first we establishes a connection, use it and then release it. In connection-oriented services, the data packets are delivered to the receiver in the same order in which they have been sent by the sender.

It can be done in either two ways : Circuit Switched Connection – A dedicated physical path or a circuit is established between the communicating nodes and then data stream is transferred.

Virtual Circuit Switched Connection – The data stream is transferred over a packet switched network, in such a way that it seems to the user that there is a dedicated path from the sender to the receiver. A virtual path is established here. While, other connections may also be using the same path.

Describe IPv4 protocol with neat diagram

IP stands for **Internet Protocol and v4 stands for Version Four (IPv4)**. IPv4 was the primary version brought into action for production within the

ARPANET in 1983.

IP version four addresses are 32-bit integers which will be expressed in decimal notation.

Example- 192.0.2.126 could be an IPv4 address.

Parts of IPv4

- Network part:
  The network part indicates the distinctive variety that's appointed to the network. The network part conjointly identifies the category of the network that's assigned.
- Host Part:
  The host part uniquely identifies the machine on your network. This part of the IPv4 address is assigned to every host.
  For each host on the network, the network part is the same, however, the host half must vary.
- Subnet number:
  This is the nonobligatory part of IPv4. Local networks that have massive numbers of hosts are divided into subnets and subnet numbers are appointed to that.

Characteristics of IPv4

- IPv4 could be a 32-Bit IP Address.
- IPv4 could be a numeric address, and its bits are separated by a dot.
- The number of header fields is twelve and the length of the header field is twenty.
- It has Unicast, broadcast, and multicast style of addresses.

Advantages of IPv4

- IPv4 security permits encryption to keep up privacy and security.
- IPV4 network allocation is significant and presently has quite 85000 practical routers.
- It becomes easy to attach multiple devices across an outsized network while not NAT.
- This is a model of communication so provides quality service also as economical knowledge transfer.
- IPV4 addresses are redefined and permit flawless encoding.

- Internet Routing is inefficient in IPv4.
- IPv4 has high System Management prices and it's labor-intensive, complex, slow & frequent to errors.
- Security features are nonobligatory.

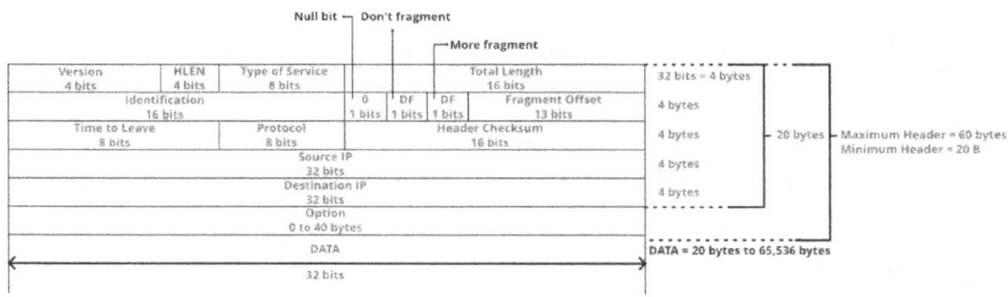

IPV4

- VERSION: Version of the IP protocol (4 bits), which is 4 for IPv4
- HLEN: IP header length (4 bits), which is the number of 32 bit words in the header. The minimum value for this field is 5 and the maximum is 15.
- Type of service:Low Delay, High Throughput, Reliability (8 bits)
- Total Length: Length of header + Data (16 bits), which has a minimum value 20 bytes and the maximum is 65,535 bytes.
- Identification: Unique Packet Id for identifying the group of fragments of a single IP datagram (16 bits)
- Flags: 3 flags of 1 bit each : reserved bit (must be zero), do not fragment flag, more fragments flag (same order)
- Fragment Offset: Represents the number of Data Bytes ahead of the particular fragment in the particular Datagram. Specified in terms of number of 8 bytes, which has the maximum value of 65,528 bytes.
- Time to live: Datagram's lifetime (8 bits), It prevents the datagram to loop through the network by restricting the number of Hops taken by a Packet before delivering to the Destination.
- Protocol: Name of the protocol to which the data is to be passed (8 bits)
- Header Checksum: 16 bits header checksum for checking errors in the datagram header
- Source IP address: 32 bits IP address of the sender
- Destination IP address: 32 bits IP address of the receiver

- Option: Optional information such as source route, record route. Used by the Network administrator to check whether a path is working or not.

What is routing? Explain the principles briefly:

Routing is the process of selecting a path for traffic in a network or between or across multiple networks
There are three kinds of routing:
1. Static routing – Static routing requires us to manually add routes to the routing table.
Advantages –

- Because there is no routing overhead for the router CPU, a less expensive router can be used for routing.
- It increases security because only an administrator can allow routing to specific networks.
- There is no bandwidth usage between routers.

Disadvantage –

- For a large network, administrators must manually enter each route for the network into the routing table on each router.
- topology's routes.

2. Default Routing – This is the method in which the router is set up to send all packets to a single router (next hop). It makes no difference to which network the packet belongs to; it is forwarded to the router that is set to default routing. It is typically used in conjunction with stub routers. A stub router is one that only has one route to all other networks.
3. Dynamic Routing – Dynamic routing automatically adjusts routes based on the current state of the route in the routing table. Protocols are used in dynamic routing to discover network destinations and the routes that will take them there. The best examples of dynamic routing protocols are RIP and OSPF

- A dynamic protocol has the following characteristics:

- The routers should have the same dynamic protocol running in order to exchange routes.
- When a router finds a change in the topology then the router advertises it to all other routers.

Advantages –

- Easy to configure.
- More effective at selecting the best route to a destination remote network and also for discovering remote network.

Disadvantage –

- Consumes more bandwidth for communicating with other neighbors.
- Less secure than static routing.

List out routing protocols.

- Routing information protocol (RIP)
- Interior gateway protocol (IGRP)
- Enhanced interior gateway routing protocol (EIGRP)
- Open shortest path first (OSPF)
- Exterior Gateway Protocol (EGP)
- Border gateway protocol (BGP)
- Immediate system-to-immediate system (IS-IS)

Explain Distance-Vector routing algorithm.

A distance-vector routing (DVR) protocol requires a router to notify its neighbours of topology changes on a regular basis. Previously known as the ARPANET routing algorithm (or known as Bellman-Ford algorithm).

Bellman Ford Fundamentals – Each router keeps a Distance Vector table that contains the distance between itself and ALL potential destination nodes. Distances based on a chosen metric are computed using information from the distance vectors of the neighbours.

Information kept by DV router -

- Each router has an ID
- Associated with each link connected to a router,
- there is a link cost (static or dynamic).
- Intermediate hops

Distance Vector Table Initialization -

- Distance to itself = 0
- Distance to ALL other routers = infinity number.

Distance Vector Algorithm –

1. A router transmits its distance vector to each of its neighbors in a routing packet.
2. Each router receives and saves the most recently received distance vector from each of its neighbors.
3. A router recalculates its distance vector when:

   - It receives a distance vector from a neighbor containing different information than before.
   - It discovers that a link to a neighbor has gone down.

The DV calculation is based on minimizing the cost to each destination
$Dx(y)$ = Estimate of least cost from x to y
$C(x,v)$ = Node x knows cost to each neighbor v
$Dx = [Dx(y): y \in N]$ = Node x maintains distance vector
Node x also maintains its neighbors' distance vectors,For each neighbor v, x maintains $Dv = [Dv(y): y \in N]$
Advantages of Distance Vector routing –

- It is simpler to configure and maintain than link state routing.

Disadvantages of Distance Vector routing –

- It converges more slowly than the link state.
- It is threatened by the count-to-infinity problem.

- Because a hop count change must be propagated to all routers and processed on each router, it generates more traffic than the link state. Even if there are no changes in the network topology, hop count updates occur on a regular basis, resulting in bandwidth-wasting broadcasts.
- Distance vector routing produces larger routing tables than link state routing in larger networks because each router must be aware of all other routers. This can also cause WAN link congestion.

Explain Link-state routing algorithm.

Link state routing is a technique in which each router in the network shares its knowledge of its neighborhood with every other router in the network.

The three keys to understanding the Link State Routing algorithm are as follows:

- Knowledge about the neighborhood: Knowledge of the surrounding area: Instead of sending its routing table, a router only sends information about its immediate surroundings. To other routers, a router broadcasts its identity and the cost of its directly attached links.
- Flooding: Flooding occurs when each router sends data to every other router on the network except its neighbours. Flooding is the name given to this process. When a router receives a packet, it sends copies to all of its neighbours. Finally, each router receives a duplicate of the same data.
- Information sharing: A router sends the information to every other router only when the change occurs in the information.

  Link State Routing has two phases:
  Reliable Flooding

- Initial state: Each node knows the cost of its neighbors.
- Final state: Each node knows the entire graph.

  Route Calculation: Each node uses Dijkstra's algorithm on the graph to calculate the optimal routes to all nodes.

- The Link state routing algorithm is also known as Dijkstra's algorithm which is used to find the shortest path from one node to every other node in the network.

- The Dijkstra's algorithm is an iterative, and it has the property that after k^{th} iteration of the algorithm, the least cost paths are well known for k destination nodes. Let's describe some notations:
- c(i , j): Link cost from node i to node j. If i and j nodes are not directly linked, then c(i , j) = ∞.
- D(v): It defines the cost of the path from source code to destination v that has the least cost currently.
- P(v): It defines the previous node (neighbor of v) along with current least cost path from source to v.
- N: It is the total number of nodes available in the network.

Algorithm: Initialization
N = {A} // A is a root node.
for all nodes v
if v adjacent to A
then D(v) = c(A,v)
else D(v) = infinity
loop
find w not in N such that D(w) is a minimum.
Add w to N
Update D(v) for all v adjacent to w and not in N:
D(v) = min(D(v) , D(w) + c(w,v))
Until all nodes in N

In the above algorithm, an initialization step is followed by the loop. The number of times the loop is executed is equal to the total number of nodes available in the network.

Briefly explain RIP protocol.

Routing Information Protocol is a dynamic routing protocol that finds the best path between the source and destination networks by using hop count as a routing metric. It is a distance-vector routing protocol with an AD value of 120 that operates on the OSI model's Network layer. The port number 520 is used by RIP.

Hop Count: The number of routers that occur between the source and destination networks is referred to as the hop count.

The path with the fewest hops is deemed the best route to a network and is thus added to the routing table.

RIP avoids routing loops by limiting the number of hops between the source and destination.

The maximum hop count for RIP is 15, and a hop count of 16 indicates that the network is unreachable.

Features of RIP

1. Updates of the network are exchanged periodically.

2. Updates (routing information) are always broadcast.

3. Full routing tables are sent in updates.

4. Routers always trust routing information received from neighbor routers. This is also known as *Routing on* rumors.

RIP versions :

There are three versions of routing information protocol – RIP Version1, RIP Version2, and RIPng.

RIP Version1	RIP Version2	RIPng
Sends update as broadcast	Sends update as multicast	Sends update as multicast
Broadcast at 255.255.255.255	Multicast at 224.0.0.9	Multicast at FF02::9 (RIPng can only run on IPv6 networks)
Doesn't support authentication of updated messages	Supports authentication of RIPv2 update messages	–
Classful routing protocol	Classless protocol updated supports classful	Classless updates are sent

RIP Versions

RIP v1 is known as *Classful* Routing Protocol because it doesn't send information of subnet mask in its routing update.

RIP v2 is known as *Classless* Routing Protocol because it sends information of the subnet mask in its routing update.

Briefly explain OSPF protocol.

- Open Shortest Path First (OSPF) is a link-state routing protocol that uses its own Shortest Path First algorithm to find the best path between the source and destination routers.
- OSPF is a protocol developed by the Internet Engineering Task Force (IETF) as part of the Interior Gateway Protocol (IGP), which is a network layer protocol that operates on protocol 89 and employs AD value 110, and have the aim to move packets within a large autonomous system or routing domain.
- OSPF communicates using the multicast address 224.0.0.5 for normal communication and 224.0.0.6 for updates to the designated router (DR)/Backup Designated Router (BDR).

OSPF terms – Router I'd – It is the router's most recent active IP address. The highest loopback address is considered first. If no loopback is configured, the highest active IP address on the router's interface is used.

1. Router priority – It is an 8-bit value assigned to a router operating OSPF, used to elect DR and BDR in a broadcast network.
2. Designated Router (DR) – It is chosen to reduce the number of adjacencies formed. The LSAs are distributed to all other routers by DR. In a broadcast network, the DR is chosen, and all other routers share their DBD. In a broadcast network, the router requests an update from DR, and DR responds with an update.
3. Backup Designated Router (BDR) – BDR is a backup to DR in a broadcast network. When DR goes down, BDR becomes DR and performs its functions.

DR and BDR election – DR and BDR election takes place in the broadcast network or multi-access network. Here are the criteria for the election: Router having the highest router priority will be declared as DR. If there is a tie in router priority, I would consider the highest router. The highest loopback address is considered first. If no loopback is configured, the highest active IP address on the router's interface is used.

IV
Transport Layer

Explain the services provided to the upper layer by the transport layer:

- The transport layer is a 4th layer from the top.
- The main role of the transport layer is to provide the communication services directly to the application processes running on different hosts.
- The transport layer provides a logical communication between application processes running on different hosts. Although the application processes on different hosts are not physically connected, application processes use the logical communication provided by the transport layer to send the messages to each other.
- The transport layer protocols are implemented in the end systems but not in the network routers.
- A computer network provides more than one protocol to the network applications. For example, TCP and UDP are two transport layer protocols that provide a different set of services to the network layer.
- All transport layer protocols provide multiplexing/demultiplexing service. It also provides other services such as reliable data transfer, bandwidth guarantees, and delay guarantees.
- Each of the applications in the application layer has the ability to send a message by using TCP or UDP. The application communicates by using either of these two protocols. Both TCP and UDP will then communicate with the internet protocol in the internet layer. The applications can

read and write to the transport layer. Therefore, we can say that communication is a two-way process.

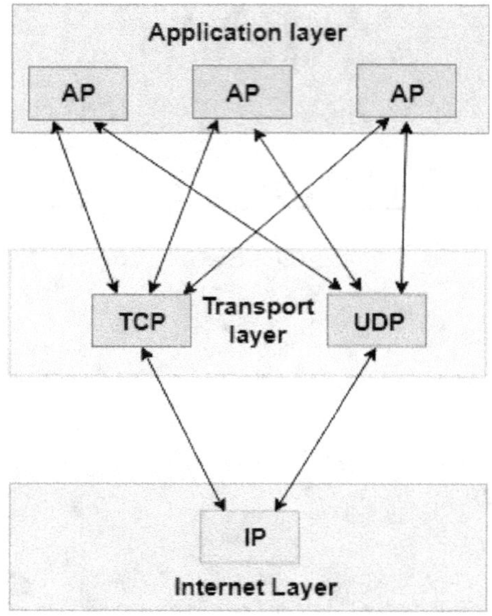

Services provided by the Transport Layer. The services provided by the transport layer are similar to those of the data link layer. The data link layer provides the services within a single network while the transport layer provides the services across an internetwork made up of many networks. The data link layer controls the physical layer while the transport layer controls all the lower layers. The services provided by the transport layer protocols can be divided into five categories:

- End-to-end delivery
- Addressing
- Reliable delivery
- Flow control
- Multiplexing

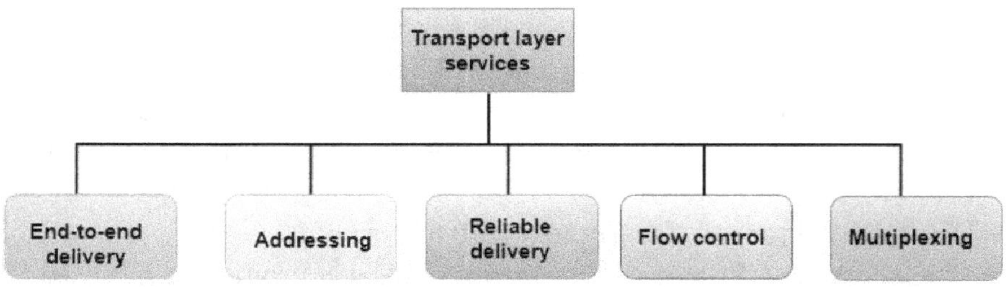

Transport Layer Services

·

- End-to-end delivery:
- The transport layer transmits the entire message to the destination. Therefore, it ensures the end-to-end delivery of an entire message from a source to the destination.
- Reliable delivery:
- The transport layer provides reliability services by retransmitting the lost and damaged packets.
- The reliable delivery has four aspects:
- Error control
- Sequence control
- Loss control
- Duplication control

Explain TCP protocol in brief:

- TCP stands for Transmission Control Protocol. It is a transport layer protocol that facilitates the transmission of packets from source to destination. It is a connection-oriented protocol that means it establishes the connection prior to the communication that occurs between the computing devices in a network. This protocol is used with an IP protocol, so together, they are referred to as a TCP/IP.
- The main functionality of the TCP is to take the data from the application layer. Then it divides the data into a several packets, provides numbering

to these packets, and finally transmits these packets to the destination. The TCP, on the other side, will reassemble the packets and transmits them to the application layer. As we know that TCP is a connection-oriented protocol, so the connection will remain established until the communication is not completed between the sender and the receiver.

- Features of TCP protocol
- The following are the features of a TCP protocol:
- Transport Layer Protocol: TCP is a transport layer protocol as it is used in transmitting the data from the sender to the receiver.
- Reliable: TCP is a reliable protocol as it follows the flow and error control mechanism. It also supports the acknowledgment mechanism, which checks the state and sound arrival of the data. In the acknowledgment mechanism, the receiver sends either positive or negative acknowledgment to the sender so that the sender can get to know whether the data packet has been received or needs to resend.
- Order of the data is maintained: This protocol ensures that the data reaches the intended receiver in the same order in which it is sent. It orders and numbers each segment so that the TCP layer on the destination side can reassemble them based on their ordering.
- Connection-oriented: It is a connection-oriented service that means the data exchange occurs only after the connection establishment. When the data transfer is completed, then the connection will get terminated.
- Full duplex : It is a full-duplex means that the data can transfer in both directions at the same time.
- Stream-oriented : TCP is a stream-oriented protocol as it allows the sender to send the data in the form of a stream of bytes and also allows the receiver to accept the data in the form of a stream of bytes. TCP creates an environment in which both the sender and receiver are connected by an imaginary tube known as a virtual circuit. This virtual circuit carries the stream of bytes across the internet.
- **Need of Transport Control Protocol:** In the layered architecture of a network model, the whole task is divided into smaller tasks. Each task is assigned to a particular layer that processes the task. In the TCP/IP model, five layers are application layer, transport layer, network layer, data link layer, and physical layer. The transport layer has a critical role in providing end-to-end communication to the directly application processes. It creates 65,000 ports so that the multiple applications can be accessed at the same time. It takes the data from the upper layer, and

it divides the data into smaller packets and then transmits them to the network layer.

.

Differentiate TCP and UDP protocol

Sr. No.	Key	TCP (Transmission Control Protocol)	UDP (User Datagram Protocol)
1	Definition	It is a communications protocol, using which the data is transmitted between systems over the network. In this, the data is transmitted into the form of packets. It includes error-checking, guarantees the delivery and preserves the order of the data packets.	It is same as the TCP protocol except this doesn't guarantee the error-checking and data recovery. If you use this protocol, the data will be sent continuously, irrespective of the issues in the receiving end.
2	Design	TCP is a connection oriented protocol.	UDP is a connection less protocol.
3	Reliable	As TCP provides error checking support and also guarantees delivery of data to the destination router this make it more reliable as compared to UDP.	While on other hand UDP does provided only basic error checking support using checksum so the delivery of data to the destination cannot be guaranteed in UDP as compared to that in case of TCP.
4	Data transmission	In TCP the data is transmitted in a particular sequence which means that packets arrive in-order at the receiver.	On other hand there is no sequencing of data in UDP in order to implement ordering it has to be managed by the application layer.
5	Performance	TCP is slower and less efficient in performance as compared to UDP. Also TCP is heavy-weight as compared to UDP.	On other hand UDP is faster and more efficient than TCP.
6	Retransmission	Retransmission of data packets is possible in TCP in case packet get lost or need to resend.	On other hand retransmission of packets is not possible in UDP.

Explain DNS with diagram:

- An application layer protocol defines how the application processes running on different systems, pass the messages to each other.
- DNS is an abbreviation for Domain Name System.
- DNS is a directory service that provides a mapping between a host's name and its numerical address on the network.
- DNS is required for the internet to function.
- A domain name is assigned to each node in a tree, and a full domain name is a sequence of symbols denoted by dots.
- DNS is a service that converts domain names to IP addresses. This enables network users to search for other hosts using user-friendly names rather than remembering IP addresses.
- For example, if EduSoft's FTP site had an IP address of 132.147.165.50, most people would access it by typing ftp.EduSoft.com. As a result, the domain name is more trustworthy than the IP address.
- DNS is a TCP/IP protocol that is used on a variety of platforms. There are three types of domain names in the domain name space: generic domains, country domains, and inverse domains.
- Generic Domains
- It defines the registered hosts according to their generic behavior.
- Each node in a tree defines the domain name, which is an index to the DNS database.
- It uses three-character labels, and these labels describe the organization type.

Label	Description
Aero	Airlines and aerospace companies
Biz	Businesses or firms
Com	Commercial Organizations
Coop	Cooperative business Organizations
Edu	Educational institutions
Gov	Government institutions
Info	Information service providers
Int	International Organizations
Mil	Military groups
Museum	Museum & other nonprofit organizations
Name	Personal names
Net	Network Support centers
Org	Nonprofit Organizations
Pro	Professional individual Organizations

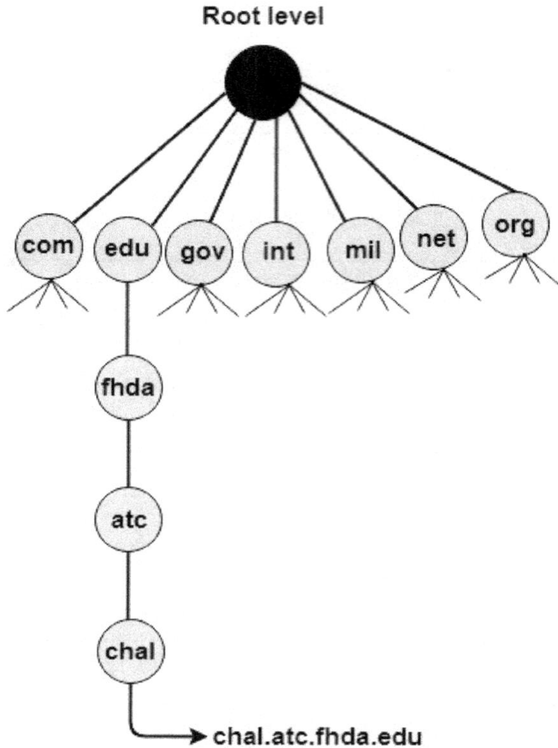

Working of DNS

- DNS is a network communication protocol that allows clients and servers to communicate with one another. DNS clients send requests to DNS servers, and DNS servers respond to the clients.
- Client requests containing a name that is converted into an IP address are referred to as forward DNS lookups, whereas requests containing an IP address that is converted into a name are referred to as reverse DNS lookups.
- DNS uses a distributed database to store the names of all available hosts on the internet.
- If a client, such as a web browser, sends a request containing a hostname, a piece of software, such as a DNS resolver, sends a request to the DNS server to obtain the IP address of a hostname. If the a DNS server does

not have the IP address associated with a hostname, it forwards the request to another DNS server. If an IP address is received by the resolver, the request is completed over the internet protocol.

• 49 •

Which protocol is used in mail server? Explain the protocol briefly:

- SNMP stands for Simple Network Management Protocol.
- SNMP is a framework used for managing devices on the internet.
- It provides a set of operations for monitoring and managing the internet.
- SNMP Concept

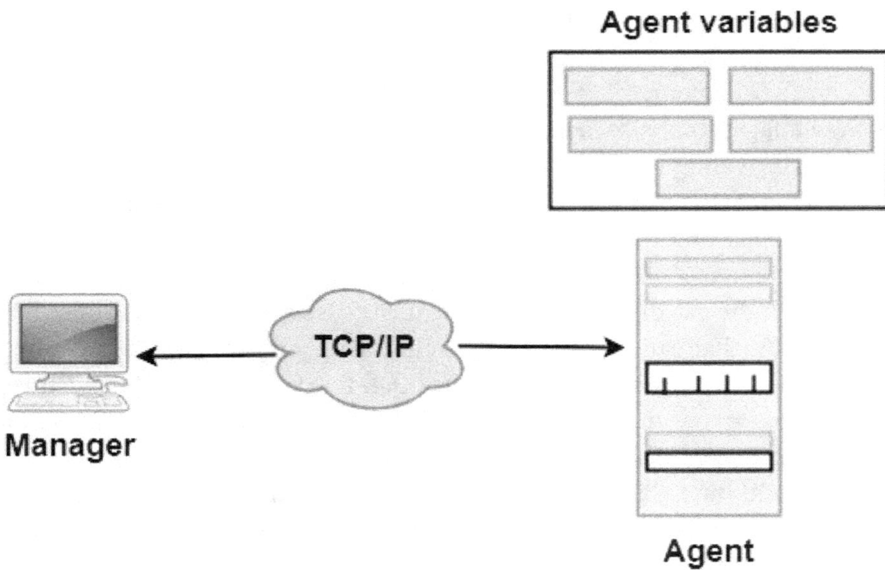

SNMP

- Manager and agent are the two components of SNMP.
- The manager is a host that manages and controls a group of agents such as routers.

- It is an application layer protocol that allows a few manager stations to manage a group of agents.
- The application-level protocol can monitor devices made by various manufacturers and installed on various physical networks.
- Managers & Agents
- A host that runs the SNMP client programme is referred to as a manager, whereas a router runs the SNMP server programme is referred to as an agent.
- The internet is managed through simple interaction between a manager and an agent.
- The agent is responsible for storing information in a database, while the manager is responsible for accessing the values in the database.
- Agents can also help with the management process. The agent's server programme checks the environment; if something goes wrong, the agent sends a warning message to the manager.
- Management with SNMP has three basic ideas:
- A manager verifies the agent by requesting information that reflects the agent's behaviour.
- A manager can also compel an agent to perform a specific task by resetting values in the agent database.
- An agent also helps the management process by alerting the manager to an unusual condition.
- Management Components: Management is accomplished not only through the use of the SNMP protocol, but also through the use of other protocols that can collaborate with the SNMP protocol. Management is accomplished through the use of the other two protocols: SMI (Structure of management information) and MIB (Management Information Base) (management information base).
- SMI, MIB, and SNMP are used for management. All three protocols, including abstract syntax notation 1 (ASN.1) and basic encoding rules, are used (BER).
- SMI : The SMI (Structure of management information) is a network management component. Its primary function is to define the types of data that can be stored in an object and to demonstrate how to encode the data for transmission across a network.
- MIB: The MIB (Management information base) is a second network management component. Each agent has its own MIB, which contains a list of all the objects that the manager can manage. MIB is divided into

eight categories: system, interface, address translation, ip, icmp, tcp, udp, and egp. These groups are contained within the mib object.

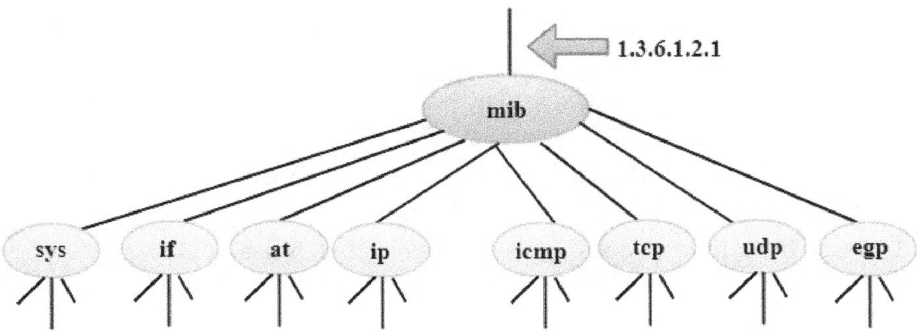

- SNMP: SNMP defines five types of messages: GetRequest, GetNextRequest, SetRequest, GetResponse, and Trap.

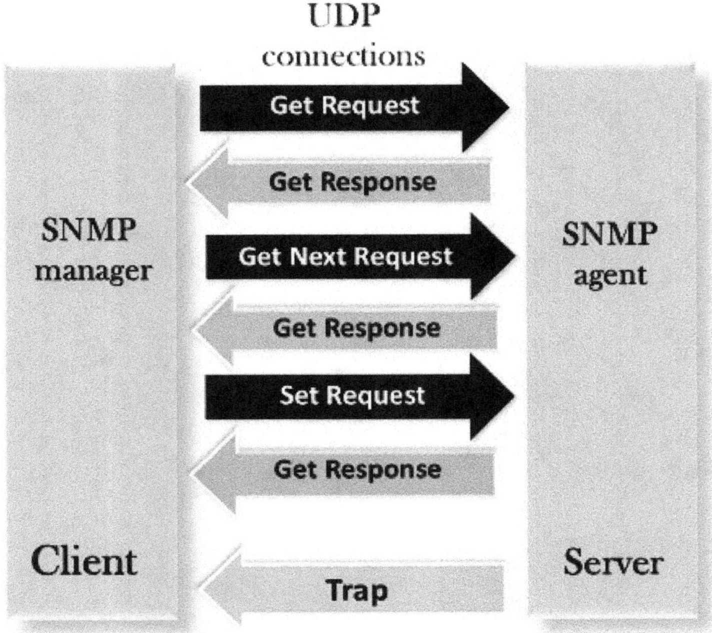

SNMP working

- GetRequest: The GetRequest message is sent from a manager (client) to an agent (server) to retrieve the value of a variable.
- GetNextRequest: The GetNextRequest message is sent from the manager to the agent in order to retrieve the value of a variable. This message type is used to retrieve the values of table entries. If the manager does not know the indexes of the entries, the values cannot be retrieved. In these cases, the GetNextRequest message is used to define an object.
- GetResponse: In response to the GetRequest and GetNextRequest messages, an agent sends the GetResponse message to the manager. This message contains the value of a variable that the manager requested.
- SetRequest: A manager sends the SetRequest message to the agent to set a value in a variable.
- Trap: A Trap message is sent to the manager by an agent to report an event. For example, if the agent is rebooted, it notifies the manager and sends the time of the reboot.

V

Network Devices and its Protocol

List out all the devices used for networking:

1. Repeater – A repeater operates at the physical layer. Its job is to regenerate the signal over the same network before the signal becomes too weak or corrupted so as to extend the length to which the signal can be transmitted over the same network. An important point to be noted about repeaters is that they do not amplify the signal. When the signal becomes weak, they copy the signal bit by bit and regenerate it at the original strength. It is a 2 port device.

2. Hub – A hub is basically a multiport repeater. A hub connects multiple wires coming from different branches, for example, the connector in star topology which connects different stations. Hubs cannot filter data, so data packets are sent to all connected devices. In other words, the collision domain of all hosts connected through Hub remains one. Also, they do not have the intelligence to find out the best path for data packets which leads to inefficiencies and wastage.

Types of Hub

- Active Hub:- These are the hubs that have their own power supply and can clean, boost, and relay the signal along with the network. It serves both as a repeater as well as a wiring center. These are used to extend the maximum distance between nodes.

- Passive Hub :- These are the hubs that collect wiring from nodes and power supply from the active hub. These hubs relay signals onto the network without cleaning and boosting them and can't be used to extend the distance between nodes.
- Intelligent Hub :- It works like active hubs and includes remote management capabilities. They also provide flexible data rates to network devices. It also enables an administrator to monitor the traffic passing through the hub and to configure each port in the hub.

3. Bridge – A bridge operates at the data link layer. A bridge is a repeater, with add on the functionality of filtering content by reading the MAC addresses of source and destination. It is also used for interconnecting two LANs working on the same protocol. It has a single input and single output port, thus making it a 2 port device.

Types of Bridges :

- Transparent Bridges:- These are the bridge in which the stations are completely unaware of the bridge's existence i.e. whether or not a bridge is added or deleted from the network, reconfiguration of the stations is unnecessary. These bridges make use of two processes i.e. bridge forwarding and bridge learning.
- Source Routing Bridges:- In these bridges, routing operation is performed by the source station and the frame specifies which route to follow. The host can discover the frame by sending a special frame called the discovery frame, which spreads through the entire network using all possible paths to the destination.

4. Switch – A switch is a multiport bridge with a buffer and a design that can boost its efficiency(a large number of ports imply less traffic) and performance. A switch is a data link layer device. The switch can perform error checking before forwarding data, which makes it very efficient as it does not forward packets that have errors and forward good packets selectively to the correct port only. In other words, the switch divides the collision domain of hosts, but broadcast domain remains the same.

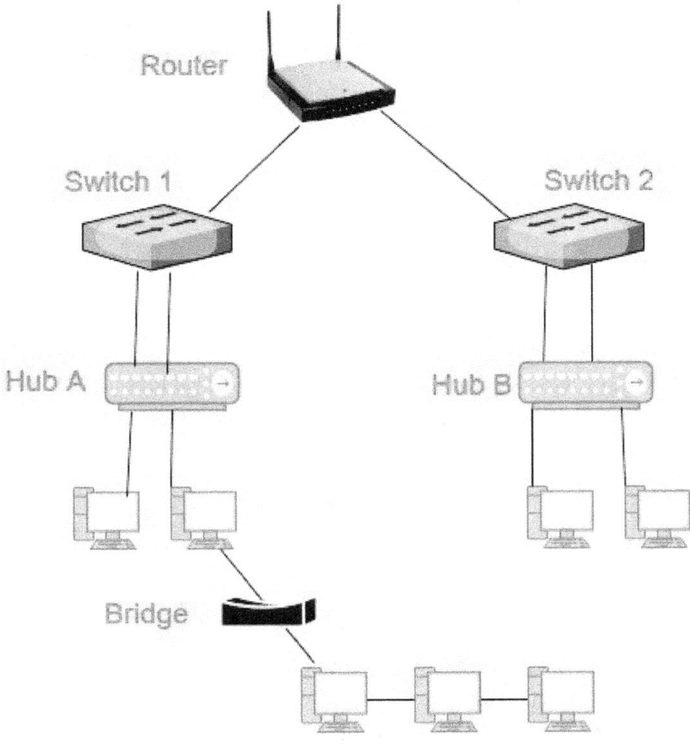

Network Devices

5. <u>Routers</u> – A router is a device like a switch that routes data packets based on their IP addresses. The router is mainly a Network Layer device. Routers normally connect LANs and WANs together and have a dynamically updating routing table based on which they make decisions on routing the data packets. Router divide broadcast domains of hosts connected through it.

6. Gateway – A gateway, as the name suggests, is a passage to connect two networks together that may work upon different networking models. They basically work as the messenger agents that take data from one system, interpret it, and transfer it to another system. Gateways are also called protocol converters and can operate at any network layer. Gateways are generally more complex than switches or routers. Gateway is also called a protocol converter.

7. NIC – NIC or network interface card is a network adapter that is used to connect the computer to the network. It is installed in the computer to establish a LAN. It has a unique id that is written on the chip, and it has a connector to connect the cable to it. The cable acts as an interface between the computer and router or modem. NIC card is a layer 2 device which means that it works on both physical and data link layer of the network model.

Explain NIC and it's types:

A network interface card (NIC) is a hardware component without which a computer cannot be connected over a network. It is a circuit board installed in a computer that provides a dedicated network connection to the computer. It is also called network interface controller, network adapter or LAN adapter.

Purpose

- NIC allows both wired and wireless communications.
- NIC allows communications between computers connected via local area network (LAN) as well as communications over large-scale network through Internet Protocol (IP).
- NIC is both a physical layer and a data link layer device, i.e. it provides the necessary hardware circuitry so that the physical layer processes and some data link layer processes can run on it.

NIC cards are two types –

Internal Network Cards : In internal networks cards, motherboard has a slot for the network card where it can be inserted. It requires network cables to provide network access. Internal network cards are of two types. The first type uses Peripheral Component Interconnect (PCI) connection, while the second type uses Industry Standard Architecture (ISA).

External Network Cards: In desktops and laptops that do not have an internal NIC, external NICs are used. External network cards are of two types: Wireless and USB based. Wireless network card needs to be inserted into the motherboard, however no network cable is required to connect to the network. They are useful while traveling or accessing a wireless signal.

Explain Hub and it's types.

What is Hub: A Hub is a networking device which receives signal from the source, amplifies it and send it to multiple destinations or computers. If you ever some across subject 'Computer Networking' then you must heard this word. Sometimes, hubs are also called Ethernet Hub, Repeater Hub, Active

Hub and Network Hub. Basically it is a networking device which is used multiple devices like Computers, Servers etc to each other and make them work as a single network segment. Hubs are used in 'Physical Layer' of OSI Model. Recommended For You: Peer to Peer Networking Model Construction Of Hub: Practically Hubs is a small box in rectangular shape which have multiple ports for connecting various devices to it. It receives its power supply from auxiliary power sources. The main work of Hub is to receive incoming data signals, amplify them in the form of electrical signals and then send them to each connected device. A Hub may contain a number of ports. Minimum amount of ports that a hub can have is 4 and it can have up to 24 ports for connecting various devices and peripherals to it. Recommended For You: Client Server Networking Model

Types of Hub On the basis of its working methods, the Hubs can be divided into three types given as:

- Active hub
- Passive hub
- Intelligent hub

Active Hub: As its name suggests, Active Hub is a hub which can amplify or regenerate the information signal. This type of bus has an advantage as it also amplifies the incoming signal as well as forward it to multiple devices. This Bus is also known as Multiport Repeater. It can upgrade the properties if incoming signal before sending them to destination.

Passive Hub: Passive Hub works like a simple Bridge. It is used for just creating a connection between various devices. It does not have the ability to amplify or regenerate any incoming signal. It receives signal and then forward it to multiple devices.

Intelligent Hub: This is the third and last type of Bus. It can perform tasks of both Active and Passive buses. Also, it can perform some other tasks like Bridging and routing. It increases the speed and effectiveness of total network thus makes the performance of whole network fast and efficient.

Applications Of Hub: Networking Hub is widely used networking connectivity device. It has many advantages over other connectivity devices. Some Application of Networking Hub are given below:

- Hubs are used to create small Home Networks. Hubs are used for monitoring the networks.
- Hubs are used in Organizations and Computer Labs for connectivity.
- It Makes one device or peripheral available throughout the whole network

Explain Router with types of it:

A router works on the third layer of the OSI model, and it is based on the IP address of a computer. It uses protocols such as ICMP to communicate between two or more networks. It is also known as an intelligent device as it can calculate the best route to pass the network packets from source to the destination automatically.

A virtual router is a software function or software-based framework that performs the same functions as a physical router. It may be used to increase the reliability of the network by virtual router redundancy protocol, which is done by configuring a virtual router as a default gateway. A virtual router runs on commodity servers, and it is packaged with alone or other network functions, like load balancing, firewall packet filtering, and wide area network optimization capabilities.

Features of Router

- A router works on the 3rd layer (Network Layer) of the OSI model, and it is able to communicate with its adjacent devices with the help of IP addresses and subnet.
- A router provides high-speed internet connectivity with the different types of ports like gigabit, fast-Ethernet, and STM link port.
- It allows the users to configure the port as per their requirements in the network.
- Routers' main components are central processing unit (CPU), flash memory, RAM, Non-Volatile RAM, console, network, and interface card.
- Routers are capable of routing the traffic in a large networking system by considering the sub-network as an intact network.

- Routers filter out the unwanted interference, as well as carry out the data encapsulation and decapsulation process.
- Routers provide the redundancy as it always works in master and slave mode.
- It allows the users to connect several LAN and WAN.
- Furthermore, a router creates various paths to forward the data.

Applications of Routers
There are various areas where a router is used:

- Routers are used to connect hardware equipment with remote location networks like BSC, MGW, IN, SGSN, and other servers.
- It provides support for a fast rate of data transmission because it uses high STM links for connectivity; that's why it is used in both wired or wireless communication.
- Internet service providers widely use routers to send the data from source to destination in the form of e-mail, a web page, image, voice, or a video file. Furthermore, it can send data all over the world with the help of an IP address of the destination.

Briefly describe Network Management System Protocol:

- If an organization has 1000 devices then to check all devices, one by one every day, are working properly or not is a hectic task. To ease these up, Simple Network Management Protocol (SNMP) is used.
- Simple Network Management Protocol (SNMP) – SNMP is an application layer protocol that uses UDP port number 161/162.SNMP is used to monitor the network, detect network faults, and sometimes even used to configure remote devices.

SNMP components – There are 3 components of SNMP:

- SNMP Manager – It is a centralized system used to monitor network. It is also known as Network Management Station (NMS)
- SNMP agent – It is a software management software module installed on a managed device. Managed devices can be network devices like PC,

routers, switches, servers, etc.

- Management Information Base – MIB consists of information on resources that are to be managed. This information is organized hierarchically. It consists of objects instances which are essentially variables.

SNMP messages – Different variables are:

- GetRequest – SNMP manager sends this message to request data from the SNMP agent. It is simply used to retrieve data from SNMP agents. In response to this, the SNMP agent responds with the requested value through a response message.
- GetNextRequest – This message can be sent to discover what data is available on an SNMP agent. The SNMP manager can request data continuously until no more data is left. In this way, the SNMP manager can take knowledge of all the available data on SNMP agents.
- GetBulkRequest – This message is used to retrieve large data at once by the SNMP manager from the SNMP agent. It is introduced in SNMPv2c.
- SetRequest – It is used by the SNMP manager to set the value of an object instance on the SNMP agent.
- Response – It is a message sent from the agent upon a request from the manager. When sent in response to Get messages, it will contain the data requested. When sent in response to the Set message, it will contain the newly set value as confirmation that the value has been set.
- Trap – These are the message sent by the agent without being requested by the manager. It is sent when a fault has occurred.
- InformRequest – It was introduced in SNMPv2c, used to identify if the trap message has been received by the manager or not. The agents can be configured to set trap continuously until it receives an Inform message. It is the same as a trap but adds an acknowledgement that the trap doesn't provide.
- SNMP security levels – It defines the type of security algorithm performed on SNMP packets. These are used in only SNMPv3. There are 3 security levels namely:
- noAuthNoPriv – This (no authentication, no privacy) security level uses a community string for authentication and no encryption for privacy.
- authNopriv – This security level (authentication, no privacy) uses HMAC with Md5 for authentication and no encryption is used for privacy.

authPriv – This security level (authentication, privacy) uses HMAC with Md5 or SHA for authentication and encryption uses the DES-56 algorithm.

SNMP versions – There are 3 versions of SNMP:

- SNMPv1 – It uses community strings for authentication and uses UDP only.
- SNMPv2c – It uses community strings for authentication. It uses UDP but can be configured to use TCP.
- SNMPv3 – It uses Hash-based MAC with MD5 or SHA for authentication and DES-56 for privacy. This version uses TCP. Therefore, the conclusion is the higher the version of SNMP, the more secure it will be.

MCQS

MCQS SOLUTIONS WITH ANSWERS

1. In fiber optics, the signal source is ___ waves.
a) light
b) radio
c) infrared
d) very low frequency
Ans: a

2. The ___ layer is responsible for node to node packet delivery.
a) session
b) network
c) physical
d) data link
Ans: d

3. The speed mismatch between the sender and the receiver is called ___.
a) error control
b speed error
c flow control
d transmission control
Ans: c

4. FTP runs exclusively over ___.
a) HTTP
b) TCP
c) SMTP
d) HTML
Ans: B

5. BSC is developed by ___.
a) Motorola
b) IBM
c) Nokia
d) Toshiba
Ans: B

6. Which of the following primarily uses guided media?
a) cellular telephone system

b) local telephone system

c) satellite communications

d) radio broadcasting

Ans: B

7. When we talk about unguided media, usually we are referring to ___.

a) metallic wires

b) nonmetallic wires

c) the atmosphere

d) None of the above

Ans: C

8. This is the ability to increase system performance gradually as the workload grows just by adding processors.

a) multipliability

b) inheritance

c) scalability

d) vectorization

Ans: c

9. PSTN represents ___.

a) private switched transmission network

b) public switched telephone network

c) private switched telephone network

d) public switched transmission network

Ans: b

10. SMTP refers to ___.

a) Simple mail transfer protocol

b) Small mail transfer protocol

c) Simple mass transfer protocol

d) Small mail transfer protocol

Ans: A

11. Class A, Class B, and Class C together are referred to as ___addressing or primary address class if the IP.

a) classful

b) eventful

c) graded

d) ranked

Ans: a

12. ___ overcame the registered number issue by assigning each organization one network number from the IPv4 address space.

a) Tracking
b) Subnetting
c) Packeting
d) Switching
Ans: B

13. Equipment that controls the physical and electrical termination of the ISDN at the user's premises is called ___.
a) NT1
b) NT2
c) NT3
d) NT4
Ans: a

14. A data channel contains ___.
a) control information
b) management information
c) miscellaneous functions
d) user data/information
Ans: a

15. QOS represents ___.
a) Quality of System
b) Quality of Service
c) Queue of System
d) Queue of Service
Ans: b

16. ISDN is an acronym for ___.
a) Information Services for Digital Networks
b) Internetwork System for Data Networks
c) Integrated Services Digital Networks
d) Integrated Signals Digital Network
Ans: c

17. Data rate depends on three factors
a) Bandwidth available
b) Level of the signals we use
c) Quality of the channel
d) All of the above
Ans: d

18. Which layer is not really a layer?
a) Host of the network

b) Network to host

c) Application to presentation

d) None

Ans: a

19. Reference point ___ is the specification for connecting NT1 with NT2.

a) R

b) S

c) T

d) U

Ans: c

20. The radio communication spectrum is divided into bands based on ___.

a) amplitude

b) frequency

c) cost and hardware

d) transmission medium

Ans: b

21. Which international agency is concerned with standards in science and technology?

a) ISO

b) OSI

c) EIA

d) ANSI

Ans: a

22. ___ blocks are identified using syntax similar to that of IPv4 addresses: a four-part dotted-decimal address, followed by a slash, then a number from 0 to 32: A)B)C)D/N.

a) IPv4 CICR

b) IPv4 MIDR

c) IPv4 CIMR

d) IPv4 CIDR

Ans: d

23. The term "e-mail" applies both to the Internet e-mail system based on the ___ and to ___ allowing users within one organization to e-mail each other.

a) FTP, Intranet Systems

b) SMTP, Intranet Systems

c) FTP, Internet Systems

d) SMTP, Internet Systems

Ans: b

24. Which agency created standards for telephone communications (V series) and for network interfaces and public networks (X series)?

a) ATT

b) ITU-T

c) ANSI

d) ISO

Ans: b

25. ___ CSMA is less greedy whereas ___ CSMA is selfish.

a) Non-persistent, 1-persistent

b) 1-persistent, p-persistent

c) p-persistent, 1-persistent

d) 1-persistent, non-persistent

Ans: a

26. The BRI is composed of ___.

a) two B channels

b) one H channel

c) one D channel

d) a and c

Ans: d

27. IP Packet is a ___ and ___ based model.

a) connectionless, network

b) connection, network

c) connectionless, datagram

d) connection, datagram

Ans: c

28. ___ are special-interest groups that quickly test, evaluate, and standardize new technologies.

a) Forums

b) Regulatory agencies

c) Standards organizations

d) All of the above

Ans: a

29. When the angle of refraction is ___ the angle of incidence, the light beam is moving from a denser to a less dense medium.

a) more than

b) less than

c) equal to

d) none of the above.

Ans: a

30. For downlinks, current design practice is to use a minimum elevation angle of about ___ degrees to ___ degrees depending on the frequency.

a) 45 , 90

b) 40, 60

c) 10, 35

d) 5, 20

Ans: d

31. The ALOHA network was created at the University of ___ in 1970 under the leadership of ___.

a) Hawaii, John Abramson

b) Texas, John Abramson

c) Texas, Norman Abramson

d) Hawaii, Norman Abramson

Ans: d

32. The term used to describe the way in which computers are connected to the network.

a) Logic

b) Technology

c) Topology

d) All of the above

Ans: c

33. FDM stands for

a) Fixed division multiplexing

b) First division multiplexing

c) Frequency division multiplexing

d) None

Ans: c

34. FDDI stands for

a) Fixed distributed data interface

b) First division data interface

c) Fiber distributed data interface

d) None

Ans: c

35. The ___ layer is responsible for resolving access to the shared media or resources.
a) physical
b) MAC sub layer
c) Network
d) Transport
Ans: b

36. Coding can be divided into
a) Block coding
b) Convolution coding
c) Both of the above
d) None of the above
Ans: c

37. Fiber-optic communication system uses.
a Simplex transmission
b half-duplex
c full-duplex
d None of the above
Ans: b

38. Complex routing strategies can be, and are, often used in systems such as ___, ___, or ___, which are sometimes used as underlying technologies to support IP networks.
a) MPLS, ATM, or Frame Relay
b) CTLNS, ATM, or Slot
c) ATM, PDTN, or Slot
d) LAN, ATM, or Frame Relay
Ans: a

39. The concept of connected computers sharing resources is called ___.
a) Internetworking
b) Intranetworking
c) Networking
d) None of the above
Ans: c

40. VPN stands for
a) Virtual Private Network
b) Visual private network
c) Virtual public network
d) Visual public network

Ans: a

Computer Networks Multiple Choice Questions with Answers

41. IMP stands for

a) Internal message passing

b) Interface message passing

c) Internal message parsing

d) Interface message parsing

Ans: b

42. Process to process delivery of the entire message is done by

a) Physical layer

b) Transport layer

c) Session layer

d) Presentation layer

Ans: b

43. Dialog controller role is played by

a) Session layer

b) Application layer

c) Transport layer

d) Network layer

Ans: a

44. Syntax and semantics of the information exchanged between two systems is done by

a) Session layer

b) Application layer

c) Transport layer

d) Presentation layer

Ans: d

45. SDU stands for

a) Service data unit

b) Service digital unit

c) Session data unit

d) Session data unit

Ans: a

46. PDU stands for

a) Power data unit

b) Protocol digital unit

c) Presentation data unit

d) Protocol data unit

Ans: d

47. Transmission lines suffer from the major problem
a) Attenuation distortion
b) Delay distortion
c) Noise
d) All of the above

Ans: d

48. If the value of a signal changes over a very short span of time, its frequency is ___
a) Low
b) High
c) Average
d) Zero

Ans: b

49. CRC stands for
a) Cyclic redundancy codes
b) Code redundancy cycle
c) Critical redundancy cycle
d) None of the above

Ans: a

50. In ___ type of service, no connection is established beforehand or afterward.
a) acknowledged connectionless service
b) Unacknowledged connectionless service
c) acknowledged connection-oriented service
d) Unacknowledged connection-oriented service

Ans: b

EXTRA MCQs:

1 Computer Network is
A. Collection of hardware components and computers
B. Interconnected by communication channels
C. Sharing of resources and information
D. All of the Above

2. Protocols are?
A. Agreements on how communication components and DTE's are to communicate
B. Logical communication channels for transferring data
C. Physical communication channels sued for transferring data

D. None of above

3. Two devices are in network if

A. a process in one device is able to exchange information with a process in another device

B. a process is running on both devices

C. PIDs of the processes running of different devices are same

D. none of the mentioned

4. what is a Firewall in Computer Network?

A. The physical boundary of Network

B. An operating System of Computer Network

C. A system designed to prevent unauthorized access

D. A web browsing Software

5. The IETF standards documents are called

A. RFC

B. RCF

C. ID

D. None of the mentioned

6. Which data communication method is used to transmit the data over a serial communication link?

A. Simplex

B. Half-duplex

C. Full duplex

D. All of above

7. Each IP packet must contain

A. Only Source address

B. Only Destination address

C. Source and Destination address

D. Source or Destination address

8. What is the minimum header size of an IP packet?

A. 16 bytes

B. 10 bytes

C. 20 bytes

D. 32 bytes

9. Routing tables of a router keeps track of

A. MAC Address Assignments

B. Port Assignments to network devices

C. Distribute IP address to network devices

D. Routes to use for forwarding data to its destination

10. Which of the following is not the External Security Threats?

A. Front-door Threats

B. Back-door Threats

C. Underground Threats

D. Denial of Service (DoS)

11. What is the IP Address range of APIPA?

A. 169.254.0.1 to 169.254.0.254

B. 169.254.0.1 to 169.254.0.255

C. 169.254.0.1 to 169.254.255.254

D. 169.254.0.1 to 169.254.255.255

12. Which of the following is not the possible ways of data exchange?

A. Simplex

B. Multiplex

C. Half-duplex

D. Full-duplex

13. The management of data flow between computers or devices or between nodes in a network is called

A. Flow control

B. Data Control

C. Data Management

D. Flow Management

14. What does the port number in a TCP connection specify?

A. It specifies the communication process on the two end systems

B. It specifies the quality of the data & connection

C. It specify the size of data

D. All of the above

15. What is the purpose of the PSH flag in the TCP header?

A. Typically used to indicate end of message

B. Typically used to indicate beginning of message

C. Typically used to push the message

D. Typically used to indicate stop the message

16. Which of the following protocol is/are defined in Transport layer?

A. FTP

B. TCP

C. UDP

D. B & C

17. The meaning of Straight-through Cable is

A. Four wire pairs connect to the same pin on each end

B. The cable Which Directly connects Computer to Computer

C. Four wire pairs not twisted with each other

D. The cable which is not twisted

18. What is the size of MAC Address?

A. 16-bits

B. 32-bits

C. 48-bits

D. 64-bits

19. Repeater operates in which layer of the OSI model?

A. Physical layer

B. Data link layer

C. Network layer

D. Transport layer

20. Which of the following layer of OSI model also called end-to-end layer?

A. Presentation layer

B. Network layer

C. Session layer

D. Transport layer

21. Router operates in which layer of OSI Reference Model?

A. Layer 1 (Physical Layer)

B. Layer 3 (Network Layer)

C. Layer 4 (Transport Layer)

D. Layer 7 (Application Layer)

22. ADSL is the abbreviation of

A. Asymmetric Dual Subscriber Line

B. Asymmetric Digital System Line

C. Asymmetric Dual System Line

D. Asymmetric Digital Subscriber Line

23. How many layers does OSI Reference Model has?

A. 4

B. 5

C. 6

D. 7

24 Bridge works in which layer of the OSI model?

A. Appliation layer

B. Transport layer

C. Network layer

D. Datalink layer

25. Why IP Protocol is considered as unreliable?

A. A packet may be lost

B. Packets may arrive out of order

C. Duplicate packets may be generated

D. All of the above

26. What is the benefit of the Networking?

A. File Sharing

B. Easier access to Resources

C. Easier Backups

D. All of the Above

27. Which of the following is not the Networking Devices?

A. Gateways

B. Linux

C. Routers

D. Firewalls

28. What is the maximum header size of an IP packet?

A. 32 bytes

B. 64 bytes

C. 30 bytes

D. 60 bytes

29. Which of the following is correct in VLSM?

A. Can have subnets of different sizes

B. Subnets must be in same size

C. No required of subnet

D. All of above

30. DHCP Server provides _____ to the client.

A. Protocol

B. IP Address

C. MAC Address

D. Network Address

31. What is the address size of IPv6 ?

A. 32 bit

B. 64 bit

C. 128 bit

D. 256 bit

32. What is the size of Network bits & Host bits of Class A of IP address?

A. Network bits 7, Host bits 24

B. Network bits 8, Host bits 24

C. Network bits 7, Host bits 23

D. Network bits 8, Host bits 23

33. What is the full form of RAID ?

A. Redundant Array of Independent Disks

B. Redundant Array of Important Disks

C. Random Access of Independent Disks

D. Random Access of Important Disks

34. What do you mean by broadcasting in Networking?

A. It means addressing a packet to all machine

B. It means addressing a packet to some machine

C. It means addressing a packet to a particular machine

D. It means addressing a packet to except a particular machine

35. What is the size of Source and Destination IP address in IP header?

A. 4 bits

B. 8 bits

C. 16 bits

D. 32 bits

36. What is the typical range of Ephemeral ports?

A. 1 to 80

B. 1 to 1024

C. 80 to 8080

D. 1024 to 65535

37. A set of rules that govern all aspects of information communication is called

A. Server

B. Internet

C. Protocol

D. OSI Model

38. Controlling access to a network by analyzing the incoming and outgoing packets is called

A. IP Filtering

B. Data Filtering

C. Packet Filtering

D. Firewall Filtering

39. DHCP is the abbreviation of

A. Dynamic Host Control Protocol

B. Dynamic Host Configuration Protocol

C. Dynamic Hyper Control Protocol

D. Dynamic Hyper Configuration Protocol

40. What is the use of Bridge in Network?

A. to connect LANs

B. to separate LANs

C. to control Network Speed

D. All of the above

41. Network congestion occurs

A. in case of traffic overloading

B. when a system terminates

C. when connection between two nodes terminates

D. none of the mentioned

42. What is the meaning of Bandwidth in Network?

A. Transmission capacity of a communication channels

B. Connected Computers in the Network

C. Class of IP used in Network

D. None of Above

43 Which of the following is correct regarding Class B Address of IP address

A. Network bit – 14, Host bit – 16

B. Network bit – 16, Host bit – 14

C. Network bit – 18, Host bit – 16

D. Network bit – 12, Host bit – 14

44. ....provides a connection-oriented reliable service for sending messages

A. TCP

B. IP

C. UDP

D. All of the above

45. What does Router do in a network?

A. Forwards a packet to all outgoing links

B. Forwards a packet to the next free outgoing link

C. Determines on which outing link a packet is to be forwarded

D. Forwards a packet to all outgoing links except the originated link

46. What is the use of Ping command?

A. To test a device on the network is reachable

B. To test a hard disk fault

C. To test a bug in a Application

D. To test a Pinter Quality

47. What is the size of Host bits in Class B of IP address?

A. 04

B. 08

C. 16

D. 32

48. Which of the following is correct in CIDR?

A. Class A includes Class B network

B. There are only two networks

C. There are high & low class network

D. There is no concept of class A, B, C networks

49. The processes on each machine that communicate at a given layer are called

A. UDP process

B. Intranet process

C. Server technology

D. Peer-peer process

50. Which of the following layer is not network support layer?

A. Transport Layer

B. Network Layers

C. Data link Layer

D. Physical Layer

ANSWERS:

1-D	2-A	3-A	4-C	5-A	6-C	7-C	8-C	9-D	10-C
11-C	12-B	13-A	14-A	15-A	16-D	17-A	18-C	19-A	20-D
21-B	22-D	23-D	24-D	25-D	26-D	27-B	28-D	29-A	30-B
31-C	32-A	33-A	34-A	35-D	36-D	37-C	38-C	39-B	40-A
41-A	42-A	43-A	44-A	45-C	46-A	47-C	48-D	49-D	50-A

1. What is Availability?

Ans. it ensure that system work promptly and service is not denied to authorized users.

2. PAN stands for __________

a) Personal area network

b) Prompt area network

c) Private area network

d) Pear area network

Ans. A

3. LAN stands for________

a) Local Area network

b) Line area network

c) live area network

d) Long area network

Ans. A

4. CAN stands for ________

a) Campus area network

b) College area network

c) Center area network

d) Close area network

Ans. A

5. WAN stands for ________

a) wide area network

b) wireless area network

c) wast area network

d) work area network

Ans. A

6. GAN stands for__________

a) Global area network

b) Ground area network

c) Gold area network

d) Globe access network

Ans. A

7. ISP stands for_______.

a) Internet service provider

b) Indian special police

c) International service provider

d) Inspiration

Ans. A

8. IPS stands for _______.

a) IN plane switching

b) Instructions Per second

c) Indian police service

d) Both a and b

Ans. D

9. NTP stands for _______.

a) Network time protocol

b) New terminal Point

c) Network time policy

d) Network term policy

Ans. A

10. SMS stands for_______.

a) Short message service

b) Small message service

c) special message service

d) short module set

Ans. A

11. SMTP stands for _______.

a) Simple mail transfer protocol

b) Short message transfer protocol

c) Small message test protocol

d) super message test protocol

Ans. A

12. TCP stands for _____.

a) transmission control protocol

b) time control protocol

c) total control protocol

d) transmission circuit protocol

Ans. A

13. TN stands for _______.

a) twistednematic

b) total number

c) trial network

d) traffic network

Ans. A

14. URL stands for _______.

a) Union resource locator

b) Uniform resource locator

c) Union relay light

d) Under relay light

Ans. B

15. NTP stands for __________.

a) Network time protocol

b) New time protocol

c) network threat protocol

d) network term policy

Ans. A

16. www stands for __________.

a) world wide web

b) whole world web

c) world wide wire

d) weird world web

Ans. A

17. The protocol used to automatically assignIP address to a newly connected host in a network is called ______.

(a) Dynamic Host Configuration Protocol (DHCP)

(b) Transmission Control Protocol (TCP)

(c) User Datagram Protocol (UDP)

(d) File Transfer Protocol (FTP)

Ans. a

18. Third generation of firewall offers_____ to prevent web fingerprint attacks.

(a) web application firewall

(b) packet filter

(c) stateful filter

(d) none of them

Ans. a

19. Who invent www ?

a) bobkahn

b) Tim berners lee

c) vintcerf

d) lady adalovelace

Ans. B

20. WWW invent in the year__________.

a) 1989

b) 1984

c) 1999

d) 1985

Ans. A

21. TLD stands for__________.
a) time limit domain
b) top level domain
c) try low level domain
d) tata limited department
Ans. B

22. URL stands for________.
a) user relation line
b) uniform resource locator
c) union relay line
d) user roll lime
Ans. B

23. ".com" domain definition is ________.
a) government
b) education
c) commercial
d) international
Ans. C

24. DNS stands for ________.
a) digital name system
b) domain name system
c) direct name system
d) digital name subscribe
Ans. B

25. communication means__________.
a) sending or receiving information
b) sending information
c) receiving information
d) none of these
Ans. A

26. The identity management system binds logical addresses to ______for reputed servers.
(a) MAC address
(b) specific programs
(c) other computers
(d) none of them
Ans. a

27. Exchange of data between two devices using some form of transmission media is called __________.

a) technology

b) data communication

c) recording

d) tracking

Ans. B

28. IPS in firewall stands for ______.

(a) Intrusion Protection System

(b) Intrusion Prevention Software

(c) Internet Prevention System

(d) Intrusion Prevention System

Ans. d

29. when data can transfer both side but at a time only one direction can send information is called______.

a) Half duplex

b) simplex

c) full duplex

d) communication

Ans. A

30. when data can transfer both side same time data transmission is called __________.

a) Half duplex

b) simplex

c) full duplex

d) communication

Ans. C

31. Telnet stands for__________.

a) Telecommunication network

b) telephone net

c) tele net

d) tele network

Ans. A

32. NFS stands for__________.

a) new file system

b) network file system

c) new file storage

d) need file storage

Ans. B

33. NAS stands for ______.

a) network attached storage

b) network access storage

c) network activity sport

d) new active system

Ans. A

34.Third generation firewalls were otherwise called______.

(a) packet filters

(b) stateful filters

(c) application filters

(d) none of them

Ans. c

35. SSH stands for _________.

a) secure socket shell

b) secure shell

c) both A and B

d) secure session hall

Ans. C

36. NETBIOS stands for__________.

a) network basic input output system

b) network bill open

c) network basic inter os

d) network bulls

Ans. A

37. RPC stands for______.

a) relay point company

b) remote procedure call

c) right police company

d) ray privacy

Ans. B

38. UDP stands for________.

a) user datagram protocol

b) uniq data protocol

c) user diagram protocol

d) user data policy

Ans. A

39. IPSEC stands for_________.

a) input second
b) IP security
c) inputsecondry
d) inline point section
Ans. B
40. IETF stands for___________.
a) internet engineering task force
b) internet force
c) intel telephone
d) intex phone
Ans. A